INFORMED ADVOCACY IN EARLY
CHILDHOOD CARE AND EDUCATION

INFORMED ADVOCACY IN EARLY CHILDHOOD CARE AND EDUCATION

MAKING A DIFFERENCE FOR YOUNG CHILDREN AND FAMILIES

JUDITH KIEFF

University of New Orleans

Merrill
is an imprint of

Upper Saddle River, New Jersey
Columbus, Ohio

Library of Congress Cataloging-in-Publication Data

Kieff, Judith E.
    Informed advocacy in early childhood care and education : making a difference for young children and families / Judith Kieff.
        p. cm.
    Includes bibliographical references and index.
    ISBN-13: 978-0-13-170733-7 (pbk.)
    ISBN-10: 0-13-170733-7 (pbk.)
    1.   Early childhood education—United States—Administration. 2.   Educational leadership—United States. 3.   Social advocacy—United States. I.   Title.
    LB2822.6.K54 2009
    372.210973—dc22   2008026842

Vice President and Executive Publisher: Jeffery W. Johnston
Acquisitions Editor: Julie Peters
Editorial Assistant: Tiffany Bitzel
Senior Managing Editor: Pamela D. Bennett
Senior Project Manager: Linda Hillis Bayma
Production Coordination: TexTech International
Design Coordinator: Diane C. Lorenzo
Photo Coordinator: Sandy Schaefer
Cover Designer: Kellyn E. Donnelly
Cover image: Superstock
Operations Specialist: Laura Messerly
Director of Marketing: Quinn Perkson
Marketing Manager: Erica DeLuca
Marketing Coordinator: Brian Mounts

This book was set in Kandal Book by TexTech International. It was printed and bound by R.R. Donnelley & Sons Company. The cover was printed by R.R. Donnelley & Sons Company.

Pearson® is a registered trademark of Pearson plc
Merrill® is a registered trademark of Pearson Education, Inc.

Pearson Education Ltd., London
Pearson Education Singapore, Pte. Ltd.
Pearson Education Canada, Inc.
Pearson Education—Japan
Pearson Education Australia PTY, Limited

Pearson Education North Asia, Ltd., Hong Kong
Pearson Educación de Mexico, S.A. de C.V.
Pearson Education Malaysia, Pte. Ltd.
Pearson Education Upper Saddle River,
    New Jersey

Merrill
is an imprint of

10 9 8 7 6 5 4 3 2 1

ISBN-13: 978-0-13-170733-7
ISBN-10:   0-13-170733-7

To the multitude of volunteers who are rebuilding the homes,
schools, and communities of New Orleans and the entire
Gulf Coast Region. Thank you. We cannot sustain this
tremendous task by ourselves.
J.K.

About the Author

Judith Kieff is a professor of early childhood and children's literature and teaches undergraduate and graduate courses in the Department of Curriculum and Instruction at the University of New Orleans. Her teaching background includes 15 years of classroom experience, ranging from directing an inclusive hospital-based child care program to teaching kindergarten through third grade. Over the years she has served on numerous state and local commissions charged with improving the quality of early care and education. She is currently actively involved in advocacy related to rebuilding the child care and education community in New Orleans following the devastation of Hurricane Katrina.

Dr. Kieff's research interests include the use of play as a strategy for learning and development and the development of advocacy skills among early childhood professionals. She is the author of several textbooks focusing on early education and numerous articles related to both early education and children's literature. She serves on various committees of professional organizations, including Association for Childhood Education International, National Association for the Education of Young Children, and the National Association for Teachers of Early Childhood Education.

Preface

*Our lives begin to end the day we become silent
about things that matter.*

Martin Luther King

Advocates are people who stand up for, speak for, and work to enhance the lives of others who are not able—or not yet able—to speak for themselves. Advocacy is often highly visible and plays out on the national or international stage. But just as often, advocacy is quiet and personal and is immediately noticed by only those most affected. Yet, a seemingly small act of advocacy, like the concentric circles of a raindrop falling into a pond, creates a ripple effect that reaches beyond its immediate purpose, joins with the actions of others, and affects the destiny of many.

Early childhood professionals are often in the position of hearing the concerns of parents or noticing a condition that may negatively impact a child's growth and development. Therefore, they have an ethical responsibility to work in partnership with families to create conditions that will foster optimal development for all children. My purpose in writing this text is to describe a wide range of advocacy activities and skills, specific to the field of early care and education, so that preservice and in-service professionals cannot only identify themselves as advocates but develop the skills needed to be effective in multiple contexts. This text is based on the following assumptions:

- That advocacy is an essential role of all early childhood professionals
- That the rationale for this role is embedded in the Code of Ethical Conduct and Statement of Commitment (NAEYC, 2005)
- That there is both a knowledge and skills base for the practice of advocacy
- That this knowledge and skills base is interdisciplinary in nature
- That effective advocacy is informed by holistic knowledge of the child and family, the community, and the field
- That effective advocacy develops in partnership with families and the role of advocate is shared between professionals and family members

- That there are common characteristics of successful advocates and advocacy agendas
- That advocacy and advocacy agendas can be both taught and enhanced through awareness, information, and practice

Part I, Advocacy in the Field of Child Development and Early Childhood Education, lays out a definition and rationale for advocacy as a job responsibility of all early childhood professionals. It also describes multiple contexts for advocacy action.

Chapter 1, Building a Case for Advocacy, describes the critical need for advocacy in the field of early care and education and draws on an analysis of the Code of Ethical Conduct and Statement of Commitment to provide an initial rationale for seeing advocacy as an ethical responsibility.

Chapter 2, Contexts for Advocacy, describes six specific contexts for advocacy activity in the field of early childhood. These contexts include advocacy for the individual child and family, advocacy for the profession, program-based advocacy, private-sector advocacy, political activism, and advocacy in the global arena.

Chapter 3, Working with Families to Advocate for Their Children, describes four conditions that require advocacy for individual children and families. The code of ethics is again analyzed and used to define ethical practice. Finally, the importance of helping family members develop advocacy skills is discussed.

Chapter 4, Advocacy for Our Profession, Programs, and in the Private Sector, describes three important contexts for advocacy within the field. Chapter 5, Political Activism, reviews the process of policy development at the state and federal level and describes how advocates can influence this development.

Part II, Developing an Advocacy Agenda, lays out the skills involved in becoming an effective advocate. Chapter 6, Becoming Informed, stresses the importance of developing a holistic knowledge of the context for advocacy and the perspective of all stakeholders. Chapter 7, Choosing Strategies, describes educational and persuasive strategies useful in developing an advocacy agenda. Chapter 8, Getting Connected—Staying the Course, describes mobilizing strategies for maintaining an advocacy agenda. The importance of networking to successful advocacy efforts is discussed. A worksheet for developing the agenda is presented.

Part III, Advocacy as Lifestyle, discusses how advocacy often becomes a part of the everyday life and teaching of many effective advocates. Chapter 9, Advocacy in the Global Community, discusses the importance of "thinking globally but acting locally" and maintaining a vigilance not only for all the children of the world but for the earth itself. And finally, Chapter 10, Volunteerism as Advocacy, describes how volunteerism can be useful not only in supporting healthy environments for children and families but in helping each of us develop greater knowledge and skills to use while fulfilling our responsibilities as advocates.

FEATURES OF THIS TEXT

Each chapter begins with "Connections," which is designed to link the reader with the content of the chapter through brief questions about their background knowledge and experience. Next, the chapters are framed with "Profile of an Advocate." These vignettes describe the advocacy efforts of an early childhood professional. The intent here is to provide a context for the information and skills developed throughout the chapter. The chapters conclude with a summary, a list of relevant terms, suggestions for further reading, and links to advocacy resources. Questions for reflection and/or class discussion are provided as well as suggestions for action-based projects that relate to each chapter's content.

PURPOSE OF THIS BOOK

I have attempted to describe many contexts for advocacy in order to deconstruct the myth or ideal that advocacy is something that someone else does—somewhere out there—in the state capitol or in Washington, DC. My message is that we all have the power and responsibility to make a difference for children and families through our own advocacy efforts. In fact, if we do not advocate for our profession and the children and families we serve, who will? Advocacy is a professional responsibility and a set of skills we can all obtain and practice in a variety of contexts.

I have painted advocacy with the broadest strokes possible and because of that I expect that there will be discussions and even disagreements related to some examples contained within this text. Is this really advocacy? Is that? That is my hope, because one purpose of writing is to inspire more research in this area and extend a much needed conversation about our important role as advocates: those who not only see something that needs to be changed but go about changing it for the betterment of children and families.

ACKNOWLEDGMENTS

My heart-felt thanks to Julie Peters, my editor at Merrill. You supported the vision of the book from the very beginning. After Katrina I wanted so much to quit writing. I had lost all the preliminary notes and the resources I had gathered. You were patient but persistent. I am thankful that you stayed with me and kept me focused on this project.

Tiffany Bitzel, editorial assistant, you attended to so many details and answered so many questions. And when the final manuscript seemed to be lost in the mail, you found it! Thank you.

I want to thank the reviewers who read and responded to each chapter: Natalie M. Abell, University of Findlay; Linda Buck, Honolulu Community College & University of Hawaii; Patricia Cantor, Plymouth State University; Mari Cortez, The University of Texas at San Antonio; Stephanie Feeney, University of Hawaii; Diane Karther, Texas Woman's University; Marjorie Kostelnik, University of Nebraska; Leanna Manna, Villa Maria College; Denise Mauzy, University of Missouri, Columbia; Mary F. Police, Quinsigamond Community College; Helen N. Thomas, Guilford Technical Community College; and Kathy Thornburg, University of Missouri. You gave your ideas and thoughts so generously. I learned much from you and I thank you for enriching the text in so many ways.

I used the early chapters of this book as a foundation for a graduate special-topics class in the spring of 2007. I want to thank the students in that class for helping me shape ideas and develop examples. They were able to actualize the role of teacher as advocate for me. They also contributed to the wealth of resources outlined in this book. These students are Allison Baptist, Nancy Dunphy, Janet Freitag, Lindsay Guidry, Paul Hall, Pearlie Harris, Leah Jones, Ellen Lowery, Jamie McGowan, Tiffany Noland, Cassie O'Neil, Caroline Read, and Kelly Touchy.

And finally, I would like to thank my mother Mary Kieff, my sister Carolyn Barnett, and my aunt Eve McDaniel. They seemed to know when to ask me about the book and when not to even mention it. My gratitude goes also to my colleagues Pat Austin, April Bedford, Reneé Casbergue, Linda Flynn-Wilson, and Sheehan McHugh. Among this group there was never an expectation of "if" but "when" the book is completed we will. . . . And now we will!

Brief Contents

Contents

Contents

Contents

Note: Every effort has been made to provide accurate and current Internet information in this book. However, the Internet and information posted on it are constantly changing, so it is inevitable that some of the Internet addresses listed in this textbook will change.

Part I Advocacy in the Field of Child Development and Early Childhood Education

Chapter 1: Building a Case for Advocacy

CONNECTIONS

When you hear the term *advocate,* whom do you think of? What activities do you associate with the act of advocacy? Can you name some historic advocacy movements?

Profile of an Advocate

Barbara Dixon is a first-grade teacher in Chapel Hill, North Carolina. During her fifth year of teaching she was challenged with a class that, from the very beginning, struggled to meet grade-level expectations. Classroom management issues had never before been so difficult for Barbara. To help the students, she developed individualized and small group instructional strategies and instituted cooperative learning and peer tutoring. As a result, toward the middle of the year, the class as a whole was working together well and making extraordinary strides in both social and academic areas. Barbara understood, from her training in child development, that maintaining this rate of progress would require a high level of continuity of instructional strategies and social expectations between their first- and second-grade classrooms.

Ms. Dixon studied the literature and research related to classroom structures and discovered a strategy called looping, where classrooms stayed together for more than one academic year with the same teacher. Looping would provide the continuity she felt her students needed to maintain their progress through the second grade. She continued her investigation of looping and was fortunate enough to locate and talk to several teachers in nearby school districts who had moved with their classes to a higher grade level. Armed with this knowledge, she made a formal presentation to her school administrator and then to the other primary teachers. When she gained preliminary approval, she approached the children's families with the idea. When the parents and the school administrator were on board, she went to the school board with the proposal.

The school board did approve the request and Barbara moved with her students into the second grade. The students adjusted quickly to the new school year. They already knew their teacher and understood the expectations she had for classroom behavior. They also knew their classmates. While other teachers were getting to know the abilities of their students, Barbara knew just how to modify lessons for individual children. Parents were comfortable, too. The confidence they gained in Ms. Dixon during their child's first-grade year carried over to the second, and they maintained high involvement in their children's education.

Barbara Dixon's actions demonstrate that she is truly an advocate for young children. She went beyond her job responsibilities, which were to provide a positive environment for learning in the first grade. She studied the issues, followed her beliefs, and worked with others to create an optimal environment for the children in her classroom.

When you think of **advocacy,** whom and what do you picture in your mind? Martin Luther King, Marian Wright Edelman, Candy Lightner? Highly organized committees working together into the night, tireless workers going door to door with petitions, public speeches, meetings with legislators, testifying before congress, and meeting after meeting after meeting, and then again another meeting?

When you think of an advocacy movement, what do you think of? The Civil Rights Movement, Women's Suffrage, the Worthy Wage Campaign, Mothers Against Drunk Driving (MADD)? You are correct in thinking that all of these people, activities, and movements are related to advocacy. Martin Luther King was one of the greatest advocates in the history of the Civil Rights Movement. Marian Wright Edelman, through her leadership in the Children's Defense Fund, is today one of the foremost leaders in advocating for the rights of children and families. Candy Lightner, out of her own grief and pain after losing a daughter to a drunk driver, helped found the not-for-profit advocacy organization, Mothers Against Drunk Driving.

Advocates do spend countless hours working with committed groups of people. They often speak publicly and many times to legislators. But there are countless other individuals, like Barbara Dixon, who are also doing the work of advocates, work that contributes to the betterment of others. These individuals quietly go about recognizing and working to resolve issues that

Advocates are often famous people who speak on behalf of children and families.

negatively affect themselves, their families, or their communities. Most of these people do not recognize their actions as advocacy and would never compare themselves with **activists** such as King, Edelman, or Lightner. There are many ways to advocate for issues that people find important. Not all require overwhelming time commitments or highly polished public speaking skills. Taking on the role of an advocate is a natural and necessary extension of the responsiblities of early childhood professionals; therefore, after learning certain skills, it may be easier than you might think.

In fact, you may have already acted as an advocate while trying to resolve an issue related to a family member, school, work, or community life. Advocates are people who, in the course of their everyday lives, recognize a problem or issue that negatively affects them, a family member, or people throughout the world and then do something positive about it. This positive act may be something as simple as calling the problem to the attention of authorities who have the power to resolve the issue. This individual's decision to act empowers others and creates a better environment for all affected. Among this group of advocates are early childhood and early childhood special education professionals. Preservice or in-service teachers, early interventionists, pediatric therapists, child care center directors, or staff development trainers—anyone who works with young children and their families has the responsibility to recognize and work to resolve issues that disenfranchise others and/or create barriers that prevent children and their families from reaching their optimal potential.

There have always been advocates for the rights of children and families—activists who have worked tirelessly to improve conditions in schools and communities so that all can prosper and grow to their full potential. But there will always be a need for continued advocacy, continued vigilance to ensure that the rights of children and families throughout the world to health care, peaceful communities, and sound educational practices are created and preserved.

Professionals who work with young children in child care programs, classrooms, or clinics find themselves on the *front line* when it comes to the needs of children and families. They see firsthand the effects of policies on the well-being of the children and families they serve. Reading or listening to the national or world news or looking within your own program or community, you will find children and families in dire need of support. You will find educational and community systems that have become so overwhelmed with bureaucratic red tape that their true purpose has become lost in a mire

Early childhood professionals are often the first to recognize a child's or family's need for assistance.

Frank Siteman

of policies. These policies may create barriers for, or even exclude, the children and families the systems are intended to serve, or they may create situations that prevent the delivery of what is considered *best practice* when serving young children. All early childhood professionals have an ethical responsibility to be vigilant of such situations and to take action to alleviate them. They should see themselves as agents of change with skills to voice, initiate, and formulate the change process (Phillips, 1998).

DEFINING ADVOCATES AND ADVOCACY

So what is advocacy, and how do you as an early childhood practitioner fit into the role of advocacy? According to Kieff and Casbergue (2000):

> Advocacy is a proactive stance taken by individuals in response to particular issues that concern them. In early childhood education, the purpose of advocacy is to promote ideas and seek resolutions that will affect children and families in positive ways. (p. 13)

The term **proactive** implies that one recognizes a problem or issue, studies the issue from many different perspectives, joins or creates a forum that promotes discussion among diverse stakeholders, and comes away from this forum with ideas and alternatives that will create a better situation for everyone. For example, Robin James, a first-grade teacher, receives a copy of the school-wide schedule during a morning meeting with the principal. As she studies the schedule, she realizes that because of the way the computer labs are scheduled, her students will not have a morning block of time to engage in center activities. Robin knows that large blocks of time for engagement in learning activities facilitate optimal learning among young children. In studying the schedule, she finds several ways to adjust it so that her students and students in other classrooms have longer time blocks between scheduled activities. Ms. James discusses her ideas with other teachers, and together they approach the principal and work out a schedule that benefits everyone. Her response to the situation regarding the class schedule was positive and proactive, not reactive, which implies a negative or nonresponse to a situation.

In the field of early childhood education, "advocacy is the willingness to take a stand on behalf of children and families that goes beyond common decency or expectations" (Jalongo & Isenberg, 2000, p. 36). So was Robin James' reaction to the computer lab scheduling an act of advocacy, or was she just doing her job—fulfilling expectations of a good early childhood educator? Certainly, we would expect any teacher to work to create a positive learning environment, and scheduling is a major factor in this environment. Therefore, as part of her job, she needed to find a way to create large blocks of time for student engagement. In fulfilling this job expectation, she acted as an advocate. She was proactive and collaborated with others to improve conditions for all.

The role of advocate is often seamlessly folded into job expectations, and therefore the skills involved in successful advocacy are skills necessary for all effective early childhood professionals. What we see in Ms. James is the **disposition to advocate,** intuitively recognizing and working to resolve issues that negatively affect young children and their families. Furthermore, advocates study the research and literature related to issues and develop well-informed belief systems that they share passionately with others. Barbara Dixon believed that her students needed continuity in the educational environment. She shared that belief, along with the information that lead to that belief, with others. Robin James was passionate about her belief that children needed blocks of time to get fully involved in the learning process. She documented her understanding by sharing literature and research results with colleagues in order to make good things happen for children.

DEFINING ADVOCACY BY EXAMPLE

The following examples represent advocacy in several different contexts. These and other contexts for advocacy will be discussed in detail in Chapter 2.

Advocacy for an Individual Child and/or Family

Janet Goodwin works as a financial counselor in a major financial firm in a metropolitan area while studying to become an early childhood educator. She is the mother of a toddler and has been learning about the importance of reading aloud to very young children. She reads regularly to her own child but has become aware that some of her coworkers, also mothers of small children, do not realize the positive effects that consistent reading aloud and rereading favorite books have. In fact, they consider the time and effort it takes to read to their children a waste, and they joke about children who insist on hearing the same books over and over.

Janet organizes a study group with several of the young mothers who work in her agency. Over lunch, they read and discuss Mem Fox's *Reading Magic* (2001). As a result of Janet's advocacy, these mothers realize the benefits of reading aloud to young children and become interested and excited about learning more. They often venture to a bookstore during their lunch break and find great treasures to take home to their children.

Program-Based Advocacy

Roberto Mikles is a second-grade teacher in a K-8 school in an impoverished urban neighborhood. The school is organized so that each grade level is grouped together in separate hallways. Roberto has found that students' reading skills are strengthened when they read to and tutor children with less developed literacy skills. However, the school's organization makes it very difficult to supervise students as they move to and from different classrooms.

Mr. Mikles feels that a reorganization of the classrooms, putting a kindergarten, first, and second grade together in one hallway, would facilitate movement among classrooms, allowing children to read with different skill groups, thereby increasing the effectiveness of literacy instruction in all classrooms. He researches the idea of family grouping and cross-age literacy instruction. He then outlines his findings and presents them at age-level team meetings. Soon he forms an advocacy group of teachers who are also interested in trying new organizational and instructional strategies.

The advocacy group collaborates to develop a formalized presentation for the principal and the other staff members to propose the creation of a cross-grade-level planning team. There are many issues to work out, but the team maintains its resolve and eventually wins the right to reorganize their classrooms, with kindergarten and first- and second-grade classrooms situated together in one hallway.

Advocacy for the Profession

Marty Willis is the director of Head Start programs in a county in rural Georgia. He is keenly aware of the need for many more high-quality programs to serve the needs of all who qualify in his county. He also knows that quality programs require well-educated professionals as teachers. Marty works with the state task force for early childhood program development. This task force is working with a legislator to develop and sponsor a proposal that will increase the funding to Head Start programs throughout the state. The proposal includes the implementation of a salary schedule that will reward Head Start teachers for obtaining advanced training in early childhood education.

As you can see by these examples, advocates are informed decision makers. They study issues carefully and form passionate beliefs about what makes for positive environments for children and families. When they recognize a policy or issue that creates a barrier to the well-being of children and families, they study the issue carefully, seeking to understand all perspectives. They then collaborate with others to determine what actions can be taken immediately and what should be done in the long term to support the well-being of children and families in question. They often form **coalitions** with other organizations in order to maintain support for the effort.

THE CRITICAL NEED FOR ADVOCACY

The early years are critical years for the learning and development of young children, and therefore it is crucial for them to receive the best possible care and education. Since it is virtually impossible for children to speak for themselves regarding their health, educational, emotional, and physical needs, advocacy is a high priority among early childhood professionals (Henniger, 2008). Family members are often overwhelmed or disenfranchised, or otherwise lack the skill and/or knowledge to lobby for the rights of their children. They need the support of articulate, dedicated professionals to speak out on issues that affect them. A position statement defining appropriate practice in early childhood states that early childhood professionals have two primary goals: first, to support the family unit, and second, to help children meet their full potential (Bredekamp & Copple, 1997). Therefore, early childhood professionals have the responsibility to become involved in issues that impinge directly on the families and children in their care.

Among the critical issues that impact children's development is the appropriateness of the practices and environments fostered in schools and community programs serving young children and their families. Parents and other community members, including many policy makers, do not always know what constitutes best practice for these populations. They may believe that young children learn like older children and adults and therefore classrooms, programs, and schedules should resemble what they remember from their own middle school and high school education. Early childhood professionals must assume the responsibility of informing the public of conditions in the school and community that foster optimal development for children (Seefeldt & Barbour, 1997).

ADVOCACY AS AN ETHICAL RESPONSIBILITY

Advocacy by early childhood professionals is not only a critical need but also an ethical responsibility. Recognizing that young children are at a crucial point in their development and learning and are unable to articulate their needs and rights, the National Association for the Education of Young Children (NAEYC) began in 1976 to formulate a **Code of Ethical Conduct and Statement of Commitment.** The primary goal of the code is to provide a "moral compass" for decision making for early childhood educators. It is consistently reviewed and revised and therefore reflects the field's current understanding of how early childhood educators can best serve young children and their families (Freeman & Feeney, 2004). Standards of ethical behavior are based on core values rooted in the field of early childhood. These values are:

- Appreciate childhood as a unique and valuable stage of the human life cycle
- Base our work on knowledge of how children develop and learn
- Appreciate and support the bond between the child and family
- Recognize that children are best understood and supported in the context of family, culture, community, and society
- Respect the dignity, worth, and uniqueness of each individual (child, family member, and colleague)
- Respect diversity in children, families, and colleagues
- Recognize that children and adults achieve their full potential in the context of relationships that are based on trust and respect (NAEYC, 2005)

The code sets forth a conceptual framework defining practitioner responsibilities in four sections, each representing the relationships between the practitioner and: (1) children, (2) families, (3) colleagues, and (4) community and society. Each section includes ideals and principals. Ideals reflect the aspirations of exemplary practice. Principles are intended to guide conduct, defining practices that are required, prohibited, and permitted. The role of advocate is implicit within the code, beginning with Principle 1.1:

> Above all, we shall not harm children. We shall not participate in practices that are emotionally damaging, physically harmful, disrespectful, degrading, dangerous, exploitative, or intimidating to children. This principle has precedence over all others in the Code. (NAEYC, 2005)

Principle 1.3 goes on to state:

> We shall not participate in practices that discriminate against children by denying benefits, giving special advantages, or excluding them from programs or activities on the basis of their sex, race, national origin, religious beliefs, medical condition, disability, or the marital status/family structure, sexual orientation, or religious beliefs or other affiliations of their families. (Aspects of this principle do not apply in programs that have a lawful mandate to provide services to a particular population of children. (NAEYC, 2005)

This implies that among the most important responsibilities of early childhood professionals are the recognition of practices that are harmful to children and their families and the rejection of such practices. In rejecting inappropriate practice, professionals need to define, create, and insist upon appropriate practice. Therefore, in fulfilling the ethical responsibility outlined in the above principles, early childhood professionals are called upon to be advocates, not just within the confines of their job but in the context of the communities, indeed the world, in which they live and work.

In 2004, NAEYC together with the National Association for Early Childhood Teacher Educators (NAECTE) and the American Associate Degree Early Childhood Educators (ACCESS) adopted a joint position statement entitled *Code of Ethical Conduct: Supplement for Early Childhood Adult Educators*. This supplement supports the idea that advocacy is an ethical responsibility for this population of early childhood professionals as demonstrated in the following ideal statements:

I-5.3 To speak out against practices that are unjust or harmful to young children and their families.

I-6.5 To make other professionals, the public, and policy makers aware of the importance of the early years and the positive impact on society of high-quality early childhood programs staffed by well-trained early childhood professionals.

I-6.7 To advocate on behalf of children, families, high-quality programs and services for children, and professional development for the early childhood workforce. (NAEYC, 2004b, available at www.naeyc.org)

In 2006, another supplement to the Code of Ethical Conduct was created by NAEYC. This supplement spells out the unique responsibilities of Early Childhood Program Administrators. It also contains language that indicates that advocacy for universal access to quality programs and for professional development opportunities for teachers are the responsibility of program administrators.

The Division for Early Childhood (DEC) of the Council for Exceptional Children (CEC) adopted in 1996 and revised in 1999 a code of ethics that also includes advocacy as a fundamental responsibility. Standard 8 states:

Serve as an advocate for children with special needs and their families and for the professionals who serve them in our communities, working with those who make the policy and programmatic decisions that enhance or depreciate the quality of their lives. (DEC, 1999 as reprinted in Sandall, McLean, & Smith, 2000, p. 164)

ADVOCACY AS A STANDARD OF PROFESSIONAL PRACTICE

Because advocacy is both a critical need and an ethical responsibility for early childhood, early intervention, and early childhood special education professionals, it is recognized by all bodies that accredit educational programs leading to degrees in these specialty areas as an important skill worthy of study and development (Hyson, 2003). These accrediting bodies include NAEYC for the Associate Degree, initial certification, and the advanced degrees of master's and doctorate, The Council for Exceptional

Children, Division of Early Childhood (CEC-DEC), for early intervention and early childhood special education, and the National Board for Professional Teaching Standards (NBPTS) for early childhood/generalist.

The National Council for Accreditation of Teacher Education (NCATE), an organization that accredits colleges, schools, or departments of education programs at the baccalaureate and advanced degree levels in the United States, is comprised of a coalition of 35 specialty practitioner associations (SPAs). Each SPA creates the standards for judging educational programs in their specific profession. NAEYC is the SPA that develops standards for early childhood professionals at the initial (bachelor's degree) and advanced levels (master's and doctoral degree). Advocacy is clearly stated as an important expectation for all (initial and advanced level) early childhood professionals in Standard 5: Becoming a Professional. "They are informed advocates for sound educational practice and policies" (Hyson, 2003, p. 29). The supporting explanation for the key element of advocacy at the initial level begins to define explicitly the skills and abilities involved in being an advocate.

> Finally, early childhood candidates demonstrate that they can engage in informed advocacy for children and the profession. They know about central policy issues in the field, including professional compensation, financing of the early childhood system, and standard setting and assessment. They are aware of and engaged in examining ethical issues and societal concerns about program quality and provisions of early childhood services and the implications of those issues for advocacy and policy change. Candidates have a basic understanding of how public policies are developed, and they demonstrate essential advocacy skills, including verbal and written communication and collaboration with others around common issues. (Hyson, 2003, p. 46)

At the advanced level, advocacy is listed as one of nine essential professional tools: "Advanced program candidates demonstrate competence in articulating and advocating for sound professional practices and public policies for the positive development and learning of all young children" (Hyson, 2003, p. 77). These candidates are required to identify and analyze public policy issues, build coalitions, communicate early childhood issues to diverse stakeholders, demonstrate knowledge of evidence-based approaches to early learning and development, and advocate for appropriate care and education for young children and their families (Hyson, 2003).

CRITICAL SKILLS FOR INFORMED ADVOCACY

Professional standards for educating early childhood professionals refer to candidates who engage in **informed advocacy.** The term *informed* implies that the practitioner's actions are derived from his or her general understanding of several important bodies of knowledge. These include, but are not limited to, knowledge of child development; critical theories; best practices in early childhood; early intervention; and early childhood special education; cultural relevance; and federal, state, and local statutes and/or policies related to service to children and families. Informed advocates continually study these bodies of knowledge and maintain a high level of currency (Hyson, 2003).

The critical skills needed to engage in informed advocacy include:

1. The ability to recognize issues, situations, policies, and/or practices that cause harm or otherwise create barriers that prevent the optimal development of young children and their families,
2. The ability to research the origin of policies or statutes and examine related issues in order to gain a holistic understanding of their intent,
3. The ability to reflect on the meaning or consequences of specific policies or statutes for diverse stakeholders,
4. The ability to locate and/or build coalitions among diverse stakeholders,
5. The ability to communicate clearly in both oral and written form, and
6. The ability to collaborate on the development and implementation of action plans (adapted from Hyson, 2003).

CHARACTERISTICS OF EFFECTIVE ADVOCATES

So what makes a good advocate? What qualities and characteristics do effective advocates have in common? "Effective advocates truly believe that just one person can truly make a difference" (Jalongo & Isenberg, 2000, p. 36). Advocates see the world as it could be and are not easily discouraged. Figure 1.1 summarizes the characteristics of effective advocates.

Figure 1.1 Characteristics of Effective Advocates

Effective advocates:

1. *Are optimistic*
They know that one person can make a difference in the life of a child. They believe that a coalition of people can make a difference in the lives of many children.

2. *Are curious*
They examine issues from multiple perspectives. They anticipate road blocks and take preventative measures.

3. *Have vision*
They see the world as it could be and commit to a task for the duration.

4. *Have strong, informed belief systems*
They share those belief systems with others within an atmosphere of mutual respect.

5. *Are responsible risk-takers*
They put themselves "out there". They understand the consequences of their actions, but choose to take the risk if it will lead to greater opportunities for children and families. They do not worry about being popular.

6. *Set realistic goals*
When they reach them, they set new goals, ever moving toward their ultimate objective.

7. *Have stamina and perseverance*
They work tirelessly and do not accept defeat as an end result, but as an obstacle to overcome.

8. *Communicate effectively to a wide range of individuals*
They are persuasive. They are able to find common ground among different stake holders and form effective coalitions.

9. *Are passionate*
And, this passion is contagious.

SUMMARY

Because of the vulnerability of young children and their families, advocacy is a critical need, an ethical responsibility, and a standard of effective practice among early childhood, early interventionist, and early childhood special education professionals. Advocacy is defined as a proactive stance taken by individuals in response to particular issues that negatively affect children and families. Informed advocates maintain a high level of current knowledge related to child development, critical theories, best practice, cultural relevance, and statutes and policies related to serving children and families. Effective advocates are individuals who truly believe that one person can make a difference.

RELEVANT CONCEPTS

advocacy

activist

proactive

disposition to advocate

coalition

Code of Ethical Conduct and Statement of Commitment

informed advocacy

FOR FURTHER READING

The Measure of Our Success by Marian Wright Edelman, 1993. Published by HarperCollins Publishers.

Giving Sorrow Words: How to Cope with Grief and Get on with Your Life by Candy Lightner and Nancy Hathaway, 1990. Published by Time Warner Trade Publications.

The Autobiography of Martin Luther King Jr. by Martin Luther King Jr. and Clayborne Carson (Ed.), 2001. Published by Grand Central Publishing.

Rosa Parks by Douglas Brinkley, 2000. Published by Penguin Books.

The Looping Handbook: Teachers and Students Progressing Together by J. Grant, B. Johnson, and I. Richardson, 1996. Published by Crystal Spring Books.

LINKS TO ADVOCACY RESOURCES

The National Association for the Education of Young Children (NAEYC)
www.naeyc.org

Professional organization that promotes excellence in early childhood. Site includes information for educators and parent, professional development resources, and legislative alerts to promote advocacy.

Zero to Three

www.zerotothree.org

Offers a comprehensive interactive resource for parents and early childhood educators on healthy development of children ages zero to three years.

Community Tool Box

http://ctb.ku.edu

Offers practical guidelines to organizations focused on improving their communities. Topics include leadership, strategic planning, grant writing, and community assessment.

Mothers Against Drunk Driving

www.madd.org

Gives a voice to victims of the violent crime of drunk driving and works to prevent underage drinking.

QUESTIONS FOR REFLECTION AND DISCUSSION

1. With all there is to do as a teacher, when and why would anyone want to take on advocacy?

2. In reviewing the examples given in this chapter, what risks did Barbara Dixon, Janet Goodwin, Roberto Mikles, Robin James, and Marty Willis take? What were the possible consequences of these risks? Identify the steps that each advocate made to begin to resolve the issue they confronted. What patterns seem to emerge?

3. Review Figure 1.1, Characteristics of Effective Advocates. There are nine characteristics listed. Which three do you feel are the most important? Why? Are there any characteristics missing? Can these characteristics be developed? If so, how would you go about developing them?

4. What is meant by informed advocacy? Why is knowledge of child development, critical theories, and best practices in early childhood and/or early intervention relevant to informed advocacy? How is it possible to stay informed about issues that affect children? Which do you think is more important: information about an advocacy issue or passion for the issue?

ADVOCACY IN ACTION: APPLICATION ACTIVITIES

1. Scan your local, national, and international newspapers over the course of the next few weeks. Mark stories related to children and families. What issues are

affecting children and families locally, nationally, and internationally? Compare your list of issues with others in your class.

2. Read several journals related to early childhood or early childhood special education. List issues that emerge from your reading. Search the Web sites of the Association for Childhood Education International (www.acei.org) and the National Association for the Education of Young Children (www.naeyc.org) for positions that relate to these issues. Present your findings in class.

3. Choose an issue that you are interested in. Begin to study this issue by searching newspapers, Web sites, and journals. Identify the bodies of knowledge or information that are relevant to fully understand this issue.

4. Read a biography of someone you believe is or was a great advocate. (There are several suggested in the For Further Reading Section of this chapter and Chapter 2.) What characteristics did this person display? How were these characteristics learned? What strategies were used to promote his or her advocacy agenda?

Chapter 2: Contexts for Advocacy

CONNECTIONS

As an early childhood professional, what contexts are you most familiar or comfortable working in? What advocacy activities have you observed colleagues or supervisors engaged in?

Profile of an Advocate

Gretchen Renaldo taught kindergarten in Louisiana. Most of her students were bilingual, but she learned early in her career that many of the parents and family members of the students in the community were not. Some only read and spoke Spanish, and others who spoke some English were literate only in Spanish. Gretchen's school had always done a good job of providing families information in multilingual formats. But as an early childhood professional, she was concerned about the infants and young children who had not yet entered the public school program. How could she help the families of these children find the information they needed to support early literacy development?

One day as she was shopping, Gretchen noticed a grandmother reading a label on a can of peas to her grandchild. She was fascinated by the positiveness of this interaction and thought that if nursery rhymes, verses, and literacy development information was printed in both Spanish and English on grocery bags, family members would have greater access to ideas and material that would help them help their children. She approached the manager of the local branch of a supermarket chain with her idea. He was intrigued and presented the idea to his supervisor who presented it to corporation executives. The grocery chain believed the idea was a great public service and enlisted Gretchen's help to research effective literacy development strategies and design the bags. The supermarket produced and distributed the bags at local stores and also at stores across the region. Families from many communities benefited from Gretchen's advocacy efforts.

In the field of early childhood and early childhood special education, advocacy is a critical need, an ethical responsibility, and a standard of effective practice. Because of the diverse needs of infants, children, and families and the wide range of programs offering services, you can expect to see early childhood professionals engaged in a limitless array of advocacy activities. "All kinds of advocacy are important in the quest to improve the lives of children and families" (Robinson & Stark, 2002, p. 9).

One way to begin to understand the range of advocacy necessary is by identifying different contexts in which early childhood professionals conduct advocacy activities. It is important to note that **contexts for advocacy** are **fluid,** often overlapping. Advocacy activities in one context may positively affect conditions for children and families in other contexts. For example, the local affiliate of NAEYC plans and implements a cleanup campaign of local playgrounds during *The Week of the Young Child*. Their purpose is to improve the condition of the playgrounds while bringing positive attention to their profession. As a part of the event, they distribute material highlighting the importance of outdoor play to children's overall health. The event catches the attention of a parks and recreation board member who then asks members of the affiliate to be a part of a planning team aimed at developing policies that would increase the effectiveness and availability of the city's recreational programs. What started as advocacy for the profession extended into advocacy for program development, thus amplifying the positive effects of the initial advocacy efforts.

Six general contexts in which early childhood professionals work to improve the lives of infants, children, and families can be identified. The focus of this chapter will be to describe these contexts by providing examples of the advocacy efforts of different early childhood professionals. A thorough discussion of each of the contexts will follow in Chapters 3, 4, 5, and 9.

POLICY DEVELOPMENT AND ADVOCACY

Even though advocacy efforts take place in different contexts, most advocacy efforts involve working with policies in a variety of ways. At times, advocates work in collaboration with elected officials, school or program administrators, or executives from private sector corporations to create policies that foster the health and development of children and families. This is what Gretchen Renaldo did while working with the grocery chain to establish the policy of printing literacy tips on grocery bags. Barbara Dixon

Figure 2.1 Contexts for Advocacy in Early Childhood

Advocacy for an Individual Child and/or Family
Advocacy for the Profession
Program-Based Advocacy
Private-Sector Advocacy
Political Activism
Advocacy in the Global Arena

(Chapter 1) also engaged in policy development as she worked with school officials to implement looping as a school-wide organizational strategy.

At other times, advocates will work to have existing policies amended or even revoked if their implementation proves to be harmful to infants, children, and families. Advocacy efforts are often needed to bring about full funding of programs that have been established by the federal or state government but without the resources available to offer them to all families that need them. This is what Marty Willis, (Chapter 1) the Head Start Director, did when he worked with legislators to increase the funding for the Head Start programs throughout his state.

What follows here is a description of different contexts for advocacy and examples of how advocates work to develop, improve, or fund policies that bring about positive changes for infants, children, and their families. Figure 2.1 lists these contexts.

ADVOCACY FOR AN INDIVIDUAL CHILD AND/OR FAMILY

Advocacy for an individual child or family often begins because a teacher or other early childhood professional recognizes a child or family is in crisis and seeks support for them. This may be the context in which early childhood professionals, particularly early interventionist and early childhood special education professionals, are most familiar and feel most comfortable because it occurs within their own sphere of influence. Advocacy begins at a **micro (personal) level** when teachers of young children assess the abilities and life situations of the children in their charge, recognize a need, and develop a willingness to do something about it. "As teachers become involved in the life of their children they may ask themselves, how can this child be protected? Enabled? How can the life of the family be enriched?" (Berger, 2000, p. 72) The range of advocacy activities in this context, as in all contexts, is wide. Here are some examples:

1. An early intervention teacher coaches the family members of a child with special needs on the policies related to Individuals with Disabilities Education Act (IDEA) so they can become better advocates for their child.
2. A pediatric physical therapist learns that the home of one of her clients has burned to the ground. She talks directly to family members, obtains a list of clothing needs with appropriate sizes, and organizes a group of volunteers to conduct a clothing drive for the family.
3. A kindergarten teacher, while conferencing with a parent, learns that this parent wants to attend a school-based family education program but does not have suitable child care or transportation. He works with the Parent-Teacher Association Board of Directors to develop child care for the program. He also circulates a carpool list among families in his classroom who are interested in attending the family education program.
4. A third-grade teacher learns that one of her students has been involved in a car accident. The child's injuries require her to be homebound for at least 6 weeks. The teacher helps the family find a middle school student who can act as a home tutor for the child.

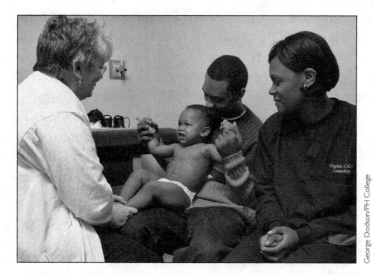

George Dodson/PH College

All early childhood professionals have an ethical responsibility to advocate for the needs of young children and their families.

5. A second-grade inclusion teacher believes that a field trip to the local fire station is a necessary component to an integrated thematic unit on community helpers. He organizes family volunteers to accompany the class but realizes that because of issues related to the medical fragility of one of his students, he will need a specialist to accompany the class. The teacher contacts the child's Individualized Educational Prescription (IEP) team and arranges support services for the child during the field trip.

6. The director of a child care center learns, via a local newscast, that the father of one of the children in the center has been killed in a war-related incident overseas. The director seeks the advice of the center's social worker and writes a memo to all personnel at the center. This memo gives center workers concrete information related to speaking, listening, and reacting to the child's grief.

ADVOCACY FOR THE PROFESSION

Advocacy for the profession involves showcasing the field of early childhood so that the public better understands, values, and appreciates the importance of the work of early childhood professionals. Advocacy work aimed at maintaining high visibility for quality programs that serve infants, young children, and their families and links their success to the mental and economic health of a community will elevate the position of the field in the eyes of the public.

The advocacy agenda in this context also includes working for the development, implementation, and funding of policies that ensure that the early care and education workforce is recognized and compensated for their valuable contribution to society's well-being. Marty Willis (Chapter 1) was involved in advocating for the profession as he worked with legislators to increase the salaries for Head Start personnel in his community.

For an early childhood professional, advocacy for the profession can include **self-advocacy.** That is, assessing one's own strengths and needs as they relate to making a significant difference in the lives of children and families, formulating a professional development plan, and advocating for the resources needed to implement that plan. By practicing self-advocacy and maintaining a high professional self-esteem, early childhood professionals demonstrate to the community their commitment to the highest standards of their profession. Examples of advocacy for the profession include:

1. An Early Start Center celebrates Worthy Wage Day on May 1 by inviting the public and the media to visit the center and learn about the opportunities the program offers to infants and families in the community and how those opportunities could be multiplied by funding policies that ensure a fair wage for those in the child care profession. (See Chapter 4 for more information about the Worthy Wage Campaign.)
2. A family child care provider decides to work toward an associate degree in early childhood education in order to improve his skills. He investigates scholarship and grant opportunities by contacting agencies within his community. He completes and submits several applications and remains in contact with the agencies throughout the process.
3. The director of a community mental health agency works on a state committee to develop, fund, and implement universal pre-kindergartens throughout the state.
4. A first-grade teacher learns that the international conference for Association for Childhood Education International (ACEI) is being held in a nearby city. She writes a minigrant proposal that covers registration and travel fees for five teachers. She submits the grant to her school's community business partner and it is funded.
5. After the conference, the grantees write a letter to the editor of the local newspaper, publicly thanking the business partner and outlining the benefits to students resulting from the teachers' attendance at the conference.

PROGRAM-BASED ADVOCACY

Program-based advocacy refers to working within early childhood programs (child care centers, Head Start, migrant education, park and recreation, after care, community mental health, elementary schools, etc.) to create environments that promote the highest quality services and education for young children and their families. Often, to maximize the effectiveness of a program, early childhood professionals go beyond their own program or school to inform and/or influence policies within the community or state. For example, a group of child care center directors lobby the

Teams of professionals will often work together to advocate for the needs of a young child.

city administration to create a School Visit Pass that reduces the price of public transportation for family members who volunteer in area schools and early childhood programs. This benefits not only the families in their own programs, but families across the community.

Advocacy grows to a **macro (social) level** when teachers expand their focus to include children and families they may not know personally (Berger, 2000). **Class advocacy** occurs when there is an effort to increase the well-being of all children and families in the community (Decker & Decker, 2005).

Informed program-based advocacy implies that professionals work with current knowledge of child development, critical theory, and cultural relevance to promote family-friendly policies and evidence-based practice throughout their communities. Advocates working in this context often find themselves in the position of educating or reeducating colleagues, administrators, school board members, or business leaders in order to retract policies that inhibit the realization of high quality programs. Again, the range of advocacy activities in this arena is wide. Here are some examples:

1. A center director decides to work toward NAEYC accreditation and begins the arduous but enlightening process of self-study. To meet accreditation requirements, many of the center's policies must be

revised. The director works closely with the center's board to educate them about the need for change. She also works with other community agencies in order to maximize the effectiveness of her program.

2. A group of early childhood teachers attend a school board meeting and testify for the adoption of literature-based integrated curricula.

3. A kindergarten teacher feels that the school's assessment system, which consists only of standardized readiness tests, does not provide him enough information when faced with important educational decisions related to retention or promotion. He develops an action research project that promotes the use of portfolio assessment. At the end of the school year, he compares the information obtained by the standardized test to the information obtained by the portfolio. He disseminates the results of his study to colleagues and the program administrator, advocating for a change in the school's assessment policy.

4. A first-grade teacher utilizes a play-based curriculum designed around centers. Several family members complain that the children are being taught as if they were still in kindergarten. She develops a Web site that documents what children are learning during center time. She also creates videos of children working in the centers and invites family members to sit with her to view and discuss what they see their children doing on the videos.

5. An early childhood college professor studies the agencies funded by the community's United Way campaign. He then contributes to the campaign, specifying that his contributions go only to specific organizations. These are organizations that he has determined carry out agendas and programs that are supportive of all children and families.

6. An early childhood special education teacher and a first-grade teacher team up to create an inclusive first-grade classroom. The teachers carefully document the development of the classroom and the progress of the children throughout the year. In the spring, they present their findings at a meeting of school system administrators, advocating for an increase in inclusive classrooms across the district.

7. A mental health professional joins a community speaker's bureau, volunteering to speak to community groups about the need to increase children's opportunities to learn conflict-resolution skills during after school programs.

PRIVATE-SECTOR ADVOCACY

Private-sector advocacy involves working with privately owned companies and corporations to develop and implement products and policies that support the well-being of infants, children, and families. Gretchen Renaldo worked within the private sector, the corporation that owned the supermarket chain, to bring literacy development activities to Spanish-speaking families in her community.

Advocating within the private sector often involves joining campaigns that pressure corporations or industries to develop family and child friendly products and services or to cease the distribution of products that do not support positive child development outcomes. This pressure can come in the form of boycotts of certain products or companies, letters to corporate executives and/or the media, or disseminating materials to educate others about the harmful effects of a company's or an industry's policy. Here are some examples of advocacy in the private sector.

1. A preschool teacher distributes information about the harmful effect of TV violence on infants and young children to the families of her students. She distributes material developed by the TV-Turnoff Network and encourages them to develop a family game night routine. She regularly sends home information about new family games they can add to their game night.
2. A group of pediatric nurses work with hospital administrators to develop an inclusive child care facility for hospital employees.
3. An early childhood center director works with his wife's company to develop a family leave policy that allows all employees 4 hours of unpaid leave time each school semester to attend family-teacher conferences for each of their children.
4. The members of a local affiliate of NAEYC join the Campaign for Commercial-Free Childhood (CCFC) and urge the families of their students to get involved with one of the many advocacy activities sponsored by the organization.
5. A third-grade teacher decides to "Go Green" and buys only environmentally friendly products. He also develops a recycling program in his classroom and teaches students why this is necessary.

6. A group of early childhood graduate students notice signs about the negative effect of alcohol on pregnancy in the women's restrooms of many of the city's restaurants. They investigate and find that no such signs appear in the men's restrooms. The students create an attractive poster and distribute it to area restaurants, asking that it be posted in the men's restrooms.

7. A college professor gives her child development class an assignment to study the issue of obesity among young children. Specifically, they are to study the relationship between a high fast-food diet and obesity. One requirement of the assignment is that students develop and implement an advocacy campaign at the university child care center to bring the issue to the attention of families and provide them action steps to avoid regular consumption of fast foods.

POLITICAL ACTIVISM

Political activism implies direct action related to governmental programs, policies, or legislation at the local, state, federal, or even international level. This action could involve working with groups to formulate legislation or policies that would have positive effects on children and families. Actions could also involve lobbying to block proposed legislation, such as budget cuts, if they negatively impact children and families.

Advocacy in the political arena often grows from work at the program or community level. An early childhood professional may become involved in improving conditions for children and families in her school or community and, because her skills and their comfort level grow, takes a logical next step and works for improvement in a wider context. The following are specific examples of advocacy within the political arena:

1. A child care center director organizes a group of center directors who travel to the state capital to testify before the state legislature about the negative effects of a proposed budget cut that will significantly decrease funding for child care block grants.

2. A third-grade teacher writes a letter to the editor of the local newspaper outlining the negative effects of a bill before the state legislature that would limit funds for library services, including literacy training for families.

3. Preschool teachers join together and lobby the state legislature to fund universal health care.

4. An early intervention teacher studies a national political candidate's record regarding issues related to funding programs for children with disabilities and decides to actively campaign for this candidate.

5. Early childhood teachers work with a senate subcommittee to draft legislation that will broaden the base of financial support for early childhood education.

6. A second-grade teacher studies the biographies of all candidates for the school board in her district. She attends forums where the candidates speak and asks each specific questions. She reflects on the information she received and, on the day of the election, goes to the polls an informed voter.

ADVOCACY IN THE GLOBAL ARENA

When advocacy efforts move beyond the confines of the United States they have entered the **global arena.** Today, the world is fast-changing and interdependent. Policies enacted in one part of the world have the capability to impact infants, children, and families throughout the world. Complex issues such as human rights, extreme poverty, war and armed conflict, and global warming require collaborative efforts for resolution. Early childhood professionals from all parts of the world can work collectively to pressure governments to work together to make the world a better place for its children. The following examples demonstrate how early childhood professionals are active in the global arena:

1. A third-grade teacher studies the educational material sent to him by a worldwide agency that uses contributions to buy farm animals for families in developing countries. She shares information with her students, and together they develop a fund-raising project and earn enough money to buy a goat for a family in a developing country.

2. A kindergarten teacher shares information about the United Nations Convention of the Rights of Children with her colleagues. Together, they write a letter to their congressman urging the United States to ratify the work of this convention.

3. A child care center director learns that a certain company's manufacturing plants are having an adverse effect on the environment of a developing country, putting children and families at risk. He begins a campaign among other child care center directors to boycott this company's products.

4. A first-grade teacher joins the ACEI forum on international issues related to children and families and increases her knowledge about conditions in the world. She learns that the United States is about to grant financial aid to a country whose policies support the existence of sweatshops where young children work long hours under adverse conditions. She joins an online advocacy campaign to notify legislators of this practice and asks them not to vote to provide aid to this country until they change their policies.

SUMMARY

Early childhood professionals, acting as advocates, work in many contexts to bring about changes that empower infants, children, and families. Becoming an advocate is a lifelong journey. It begins when professionals become interested in the welfare of an individual child or family, and it continues as advocates hone their skills and widen their personal sphere of influence. Advocacy is both a natural and a necessary role for early childhood educators as they share their knowledge about the needs of children and families, speak out about local and worldwide conditions, and work to resolve complex issues that impact the development and well-being of all children and families.

RELEVANT CONCEPTS

contexts for advocacy

fluid

micro (personal) level

advocacy for the profession

self-advocacy

program-based advocacy

macro (social) advocacy

class advocacy

private-sector advocacy

political activism

global arena

FOR FURTHER READING

Lighting the Way: Nine Women Who Changed Modern America by Karenna Gore Schiff, 2005. Published by Miramax Books.

Lanterns: A Memoir of Mentors by Marian Wright Edelman, 2000. Published by HarperCollins Books.

The Power of One: Daisy Bates and the Little Rock Nine by Judith Bloom Fradin and Dennis Brindell Fradin, 2004. Published by Clarion Books.

I Can Make a Difference: A Treasury to Inspire Our Children by Marian Wright Edelman and Mark McVeigh (Eds.), 2005. Published by HarperCollins Books.

LINKS TO ADVOCACY RESOURCES

The Association of Childhood Education

www.acei.org

An international professional organization that supports advocacy efforts through committee work and publications.

Global Early Intervention Network

www.atsweb.neu.edu/cp/ei

An online information resource and discussion community helping parents, service providers, students, faculty and others learn more about early intervention.

The National Children's Advocacy Center

www.nationalcac.org

A nonprofit organization that provides training, prevention, intervention, and treatment services to fight child abuse and neglect.

QUESTIONS FOR REFLECTION AND DISCUSSION

1. At this point in time, with which of the contexts for advocacy described in this chapter are you the most familiar? The least? Which are you most interested in? Reflect on the reason for your answer and describe ways that you could increase your familiarity with different contexts and issues.

2. Compare the examples of advocacy activities described in the different contexts. Find several that seem to cross from one context to another. Explain the fluid nature of advocacy.

3. Are Gretchen Renaldo's actions advocacy or just a professional responsibility? What about Barbara Dixon (Chapter 1)? How do you determine what is advocacy and what is a job responsibility? Discuss this issue as it relates to other examples of advocacy described in this chapter.

4. Refer to "Critical Skills for Informed Advocacy" and "Characteristics of Effective Advocates" in Chapter 1. Choose several examples of advocacy activities described in this chapter and discuss the skills and characteristics the advocate possessed or used to effect change.

ADVOCACY IN ACTION: APPLICATION ACTIVITIES

1. Create an Issues Journal. Revisit the list of advocacy issues you developed as you finished the last chapter. Identify three issues that are particularly interesting to you. Create a section in your journal for each issue. Describe, in your own words, what the issue is and why it is important. Find one Web site that pertains to each of your three issues. Take notes on the information you get from these Web sites. What aspect of the issue catches your attention?

2. For each of the issues you have identified list two or three advocacy actions that would positively impact children and families. What context or contexts does work in this issue involve?

3. Interview the human resource manager of a company in your community. Or invite this person to be a guest speaker in your college class. Ask her to discuss the value of family-friendly policies her company offers and outline the process involved in developing these policies. Discuss other policies that might be implemented and ask the human resource manager to comment on their feasibility.

Chapter 3: Working with Families to Advocate for Their Children

CONNECTIONS

Do you know of a child or family in need of some kind of assistance but did not know exactly what to do to help them? Are you aware of the services in your community that are available for families in crisis? What is your responsibility if you suspect child abuse?

Profile of an Advocate

Adrian Beneatau is a teacher in the infant-toddler program at an employer-sponsored comprehensive child care center in Indianapolis, Indiana. Adrian works to develop crucial partnerships with the families of the children in her care. She visits informally with parents each day as they escort their children to and from the program. The center has an open-door policy, and because family members work close by, they often visit their children during the day, especially at snack time or lunch. Adrian takes this opportunity to learn about the families and how they view their children's accomplishments. She has regular conferences with family members and generally begins the conference by asking if they have particular concerns about the child's development.

It was during such a conference that the mother of an 18-month-old toddler, Brianna Johnson, shared her concern about her daughter's speech development. Adrian had recognized, through informal observation and checklist assessments, early signs of a general delay in both motor and speech development. Brianna's mother shared information with Adrian about techniques she used at home to elicit more speech. Adrian made notes so that she could use these techniques in the classroom. She also obtained Mrs. Johnson's permission to share this information with the center's social worker, who would then refer Brianna for further testing.

Adrian shared Mrs. Johnson's concerns about her daughter's development and the results of her own informal assessments with Janice Black, the program's social worker. Janice called the local agency affiliated with Child Find, a nationwide program focused on identifying children who may be at risk for developmental delays, assessing the degree of the delays, and, when warranted, linking the family with early intervention services. Over the next few weeks a psychologist, speech pathologist, and both an occupational and a physical therapist evaluated Brianna's development through center-based activities, observations in the home, and interviews with Brianna's family members aimed at assessing the family's strengths and resources. Adrian also continued to document Brianna's language and motor development and visited with family members to learn more about how to help Brianna at the center.

The cumulative results of all evaluations demonstrated that Brianna had significant developmental delays in the area of speech and language, but delays in the motor area were not significant. Fortunately, Brianna was not yet showing significant delays in the cognitive area, but this was an area of concern because of the developmental interdependence of cognition, speech, and language. It was feared that, without intervention of some sort, Brianna would exhibit cognitive delays in the near future.

The evaluation team, along with Mr. and Mrs. Johnson, Brianna's grand-mother, Adrian, and Janice Black, attended a collaborative meeting and formu-lated an Individual Family Service Plan (IFSP) that outlined both the center's and the family's roles as they related to fostering Brianna's development. The plan included the family's goals for Brianna and an outline of educational goals and services needed to support Brianna and her family. Janice Black assisted the family in locating, applying for, and coordinating services offered by different community agencies. Brianna received speech and language ther-apy at school. In addition, Adrian received training related to developing a classroom environment that would support language and speech develop-ment. Brianna's family members received education and training so they would know how best to create an environment that supported not only Brianna's development but also the development of all children in the family.

Adrian continued to monitor Brianna's development and communicated on a regular basis with her family concerning Brianna's progress at home and at school. Janice also communicated frequently with the family to coordinate and integrate the services being provided. Through the successful advocacy efforts of Adrian Beneatau and Janice Black, working in partnership with the Johnson family, Brianna's speech and language improved, and by the time she entered kindergarten, she was functioning in the normal range of development in all areas and was ready and able to take full advantage of all learning opportunities.

Early childhood educators are often the first professionals to work with a family or child on a daily basis and over a sustained period of time. Consequently, they are in a position to hear the concerns of family members or notice early signs of health issues or disabilities that may impact negatively on a child's growth and development (Gonzalez-Mena, 2007). Or, they may learn from family members about adverse conditions resulting from economic hardship, family crisis, abuse, or neglect that could impede the child's growth, development, and learning. When these situations arise, advocacy may be necessary to speak for the child or to support the family so they can obtain the resources necessary to foster the optimal growth and development of their child.

In this chapter we will discuss issues relating to advocating for an individual child or family. These issues include using the Code of Ethical Conduct and Statement of Commitment (NAEYC, 2005) as a foundation for developing advocacy practices, recognizing conditions that call for advocacy, conferencing with families and making referrals, and finally, supporting parents and other family members as they become advocates for themselves and their children.

ETHICAL GUIDELINES FOR ADVOCACY PRACTICE

Early childhood is a critical period for the development of many essential skills and dispositions necessary for optimal growth, development, and learning. Recognizing when developmental or environmental factors negatively affect an infant or young child's growth and learning is one critical responsibility of early childhood professionals. Another is to speak for the child and support the family's efforts to obtain needed resources and services. Some may question whether Adrian Beneatau and Janice Black were merely doing their job when they recognized Brianna's speech and language delay and worked with her family to get the help needed or were they engaging in advocacy activities. The answer is that they were doing both seamlessly. To try to draw a clear line between what is a job responsibility and what is advocacy is to miss the point that advocacy is clearly established, through the Code of Ethical Conduct and Statement of Commitment (NAEYC, 2005) as a role teachers fulfill as part of their job expectations. The better question to ask here is how does the code inform advocacy practice? That is, can we find guidelines within the Code of Ethics that show us just how to engage in effective advocacy for individual children and their families?

In Chapter 1 we introduced the NAEYC Code of Ethical Conduct and Statement of Commitment and discussed the relationship between the code and the responsibility to recognize practices and policies that were harmful to children and families, reject them, and advocate for policies and practices that better supported children and families. Further study of the code reveals that Adrian and Janice were putting into practice many of the core values, ideals, and principles outlined in Section I and Section II of the code as they partnered with the Johnson family and advocated for intervention services for Brianna.

To illustrate the connection between the code and guidelines for effective advocacy, let's examine how the activities of the professionals featured in the opening vignette correspond to the values, ideals, and principles listed in the code. We will first look at the core values, which are the commitments held by a profession that are "consciously and knowingly embraced by its practitioners because they make a contribution to society" (Feeney & Freeman, 1999, p. 99). Figure 3.1 demonstrates how several of the core values correspond with the actions described in the vignette.

Ideals reflect the aspiration of practitioners and describe how early childhood educators should conduct their professional relationships (Feeney & Freeman, 1999). Figure 3.2 demonstrates how several of the ideals listed in the code correspond with the action of professionals described in the vignette. Notice that a consistent set of professional behaviors is developing.

Principles are the rules of the profession that guide conduct and "identify practices that are required, permitted, or prohibited by the code" (Feeney & Freeman, 1999, p. 36). Figure 3.3 demonstrates how several of the principles correspond with the actions of the professionals described in the vignette.

The Code of Ethical Conduct and Statement of Commitment not only establishes advocacy as a professional responsibility but also identifies practices to follow when advocating for individuals and families and

Figure 3.1 Core Values as Guidelines for Advocacy

Core Value: Base our work on knowledge of how children develop and learn.
> *Adrian conducted informal assessments of all children's development and compared it to appropriate norms.*
> *The evaluation team understood the reciprocal nature of developmental domains and that a delay in language and speech would likely lead to a delay in cognition. Intervention was necessary to prevent further developmental delays.*

Core Value: Appreciate and support the bond between the child and family.
> *The center had an open-door policy that welcomed family members at all times.*
> *Adrian took every opportunity to learn about her children through their families.*
> *Assessment and intervention activities involved family members and took place at the child's home as well as in the center.*
> *Family members were involved in developing goals for their child and had an active role in fostering her development.*

Core Value: Recognize that children are best understood and supported in the context of family, culture, community, and society.
> *Adrian and the Johnson family shared information consistently.*
> *Assessment and intervention activities involved family members and took place in the child's home as well as at the center.*
> *The evaluation team and school personnel developed knowledge of the family's unique strengths and resources.*
> *Intervention goals were developed in collaboration with the Johnson family.*

Core Value: Recognize that children and adults achieve their full potential in the context of relationships that are based on trust and respect.
> *The center had an open-door policy and welcomed family members to visit.*
> *Adrian worked to build the trust of the Johnson family even before Brianna's development became an issue.*
> *Adrian got permission to work with the social worker and refer Brianna for further testing.*
> *The IFSP was a collaborative effort among professionals and family members.*
> *Janice communicated frequently with the family to coordinate and integrate services being provided.*

Source: Selected core values from the *NAEYC Code of Ethical Conduct and Statement of Commitment by the National Association for the Education of Young Children,* 2005. Washington, DC: NAEYC. Copyright 2005 by the National Association for the Education of Young Children.

Figure 3.2 Ideals as Guidelines for Advocacy

I-1.2 To base program practices upon current knowledge and research in the field of early childhood education, child development, and related disciplines, as well as on particular knowledge of each child.

>*Adrian conducted frequent informal assessments of Brianna's development and compared these to well-established norms.*

>*An understanding of the reciprocal nature of development prompted the assessment team's concern and push for intervention.*

>*The center worked to develop strong partnerships with families.*

>*Janice Black was familiar with the referral process and local agencies.*

>*Family members were included in all decisions.*

I-1.3 To recognize and respect the unique qualities, abilities, and potential of each child.

>*Center personnel and the evaluation team understood that intervention was necessary for Brianna to reach her full potential.*

>*The family's strengths and resources were figured into the intervention plan.*

I-1.4 To appreciate the vulnerability of children and their dependence on adults.

>*It was understood that, without intervention of some sort, Brianna would exhibit cognitive delays in the future. The need for intervention was immediate.*

I-1.6 To use assessment instruments and strategies that are appropriate for the children to be assessed, that are used only for the purposes for which they were designed, and that have the potential to benefit children.

>*Adrian informally assessed Brianna's development through observations, comparative checklists, and interviews with family members.*

>*Psychologist, speech pathologist and both an occupational and physical therapist evaluated Brianna's development through center-based activities and observations in the home.*

I-1.7 To use assessment information to understand and support children's development and learning, to support instruction, and to identify children who may need additional services.

>*Adrian sought information from and shared information with the Johnson family on a regular basis.*

>*Assessment data was used to formulate goals and develop the IFSP.*

I-2.2 To develop relationships of mutual trust and create partnerships with the families we serve.

>*The center promoted an open-door policy that encouraged family members to visit often.*

(continued)

39

>*Adrian used every opportunity to learn about the families of the children in her care.*
>*Information was shared between the family and the school.*
>*Family members were involved in all decisions.*

I-2.4 To listen to families, acknowledge and build upon their strengths and competencies and learn from families as we support them in their task of nurturing children.
>*Mrs. Johnson shared her concerns with Adrian and Adrian reciprocated these concerns. Together, they decided to take the next step and talk to Janice Black and refer Brianna for further testing.*
>*The evaluation team used knowledge of the family's strengths and resources as they collaborated to formulate the IFSP.*
>*There was consistent communication between the family, center personnel, and the evaluation team.*

I-2.8 To help family members enhance their understanding of their children and support the continuing development of their skills as parents.
>*Family members received education and training so they would know best how to create an environment that supported not only Brianna's development, but the development of all children in the family.*

Source: Selected ideals from the *NAEYC Code of Ethical Conduct and Statement of Commitment* by the National Association for the Education of Young Children, 2005. Washington, DC: NAEYC. Copyright 2005 by the National Association for the Education of Young Children.

defines the conduct necessary to fulfill the role of advocate. These practices include:

1. Developing a trust relationship between the school, the teacher, and the family so that when issues arise, a partnership for resolving the issue is already in place.
2. Recognizing an issue or problem that may affect a child's growth and development.
3. Documenting the situation carefully, using multiple formats and contexts for assessment strategies.
4. Involving the family in decisions related to their child, while respecting their child rearing values.
5. Developing advocacy strategies that take into account the family's strengths and resources.
6. Referring the family to agencies and programs that can benefit them.

Figure 3.3 Principles as Guidelines for Advocacy

P-1.4 We shall involve all those with relevant knowledge (including families and staff) in decisions concerning a child as appropriate, ensuring confidentiality of sensitive information.
>*Adrian worked with the social worker, Janice Black, to formulate plans for referral.*
>*The Johnson family gave their consent for referral, received information from all assessments conducted, and was involved in formulating the IFSP.*

P-1.5 We shall use appropriate assessment systems, which include multiple sources of information, to provide information on children's learning and development.
>*Multiple assessments in multiple contexts were used to assess Brianna's initial condition and her progress.*
>*Information from the family was used to assess Brianna and develop learning goals.*

P-2.4 We shall involve the family in significant decisions affecting their child.
>*The family was involved in all decisions concerning Brianna's assessment and intervention.*
>*Janice worked with the Johnson family to contact community agencies and apply for services.*
>*Adrian and Janice conferred frequently with the Johnson family to determine how the home based interventions were going.*

P-2.15 We shall be familiar with and appropriately refer families to community resources and professional support services. After a referral has been made, we shall follow up to ensure that services have been appropriately provided.
>*The center had an established plan for the referral process.*
>*Adrian did her part as the teacher and then enlisted the help of the social worker when appropriate.*
>*Janice Black was familiar with the referral process and with local agencies that could conduct assessments and provide needed services.*

Source: Selected principles from the *NAEYC Code of Ethical Conduct and Statement of Commitment* by the National Association for the Education of Young Children, 2005. Washington, DC: NAEYC. Copyright 2005 by the National Association for the Education of Young Children.

7. Supporting them through the referral process.
8. Following through after referral and monitoring progress toward goals.
9. Maintaining a true partnership by consulting with the family and other professionals on a regular basis.
10. Monitoring progress.

We will discuss these practices throughout the chapter as we discuss several conditions that may require advocacy.

CONDITIONS REQUIRING ADVOCACY

One of the core values set forth in The Code of Ethical Conduct and Statement of Commitment (NAEYC, 2005) is that early childhood professionals recognize that children are best understood and supported in the context of family, culture, community, and society. This implies a commitment by those who work with young children to be vigilant regarding the conditions in which children are living as well as the conditions in which they are learning. There are four general conditions that may require early childhood professionals to engage in advocacy activities to support individual children or families. These conditions are

1. A family's chronic or temporary economic hardship that creates a need for assistance or services provided by government or private agencies.
2. A child shows signs of developmental delays or a neurological impairment.
3. A diagnosis of a disabling or handicapping condition for anyone in the family.
4. A reason to suspect abuse or neglect.

Resources related to all of these conditions are available to families in most communities. However, because service agencies are organized differently across the United States, early childhood professionals will need to survey their own community to find the appropriate provider. Many communities have developed a referral agency that can support the early childhood professional in finding appropriate resources. A good place to start looking is in the local phone directory.

Economic Hardships

All parents want their children to succeed both in school and in life, but when their life's circumstances are such that they have a difficult time providing for their family's basic needs, attention to their children's education may become less of a priority (Gonzalez-Mena, 2007). A family's economic security is vital to providing adequate shelter, nutrition, and health care, as well as a stimulating environment in which children can grow, learn, and develop (National Center for Children in Poverty [NCCP], 2006). Children who live in conditions of poverty are vulnerable—that is—at risk for developing developmental delays or health-related issues that ultimately will impede their growth and development (Knitzer, 2007).

To recognize the *face* of poverty in the United States, it is first important to distinguish between *living below the federal poverty level* and *living in a low-income family*. In 2006, the **federal poverty level** was $20,000 income for a family of four, $16,600 for a family of 3, and $13,200 for a family of 2. And yet, research suggests that, on average, families need an income equal to about two times the federal poverty level to meet their most basic needs. That is, a family of 4 needs an income of $40,000 dollars to meet basic needs; a family of 3 needs $33,200, and a family of 2 needs $26,400 dollars. Families with incomes below this level are referred to as **low-income families** (NCCP, 2006).

Low-income families may not always look *poor*, that is homeless or unemployed. In 2006, 55 percent of children in low-income families had at least one parent who worked full time, year-round, and 39 percent of children in low-income families lived with parents who have some college education (NCCP, 2006). This economic hardship may be a chronic condition, or it may be temporary. For example, a family's income can be severely affected as a result of a catastrophe such as a flood or fire, the closing of a business, chronic illness of a family member, divorce, or the death of the primary care provider.

There are several ways early childhood professionals can learn if a family is undergoing economic hardship. Family members may share this information. This is why building trusting relationships with families and developing partnerships is so important. It is the starting point of advocacy. Another way professionals learn about a family's situation is by listening to children, observing their play, or noticing signs in their artwork. For example, a child might mention that a grandparent has come to live with them and they might depict in their drawings an older person in a bed or wheelchair. They might also act out the role of a sick or helpless person while playing in the housekeeping center. Several generations living under one roof does not necessarily mean there is economic hardship, but noticing signs of such an event does provide an opportunity for teachers to visit with family members about any changes in the household and the possible effects this would have on the child. Other signs that a child's family might be in stress and need help include a radical or sudden change in a child's physical or mental readiness for the day, chronic tiredness, poor general health, frequent tardiness or absenteeism, excessive crying, irritability, and/or anger (Wright, Stegelin, & Hartle, 2007).

Many kinds of services are offered to families by both public and private agencies. These include health care, health insurance, nutrition, counseling, housing, employment, literacy education, and job training. Families that need long-term or temporary assistance may not know what is available or how to access it. They may also be so overwhelmed by the situation that they cannot act, or they may be embarassed to let anyone know about their need for help. No matter what the situation, early childhood professionals need to act with great sensitivity to help families find the resources and support they need to foster the long-term well-being of the child.

Early childhood professionals who work in comprehensive child development and family support programs, like the one described in the opening vignette, are in a unique position to help parents because these programs have staff that work specifically to refer and coordinate services among community agencies. Other early childhood professionals can find community agencies that support families by consulting the local phone book. Figure 3.4 lists federal and community programs that offer aid to families in need. Most of the federal agencies have state and regional offices.

Signs of Developmental Delays or Neurological Impairment

Early childhood (birth through age 8) is a critical period for the identification of developmental delays that may occur across all domains of development: physical, cognitive, speech-language, and social-emotional, as well as sensory modalities such as vision and hearing (American Academy of Pediatrics, 2001). Signs of neurological impairments such as autism or attention disorders often appear in infancy or early childhood. Early identification, intervention, or remediation not only improves the quality of life and functioning for the child and family, it can prevent, or reduce the severity of, cognitive, language, and behavioral disorders (Glascoe, 1999).

Accurate and consistent documentation of children's development is an essential component of high quality early childhood programs and, as we

Figure 3.4 Programs That Offer Aid to Families in Need

Federal Programs
Child care assistance
Child care subsidies
Child support enforcement income
Food stamps
Federal earned income tax credit
Housing assistance
Medicaid
State income tax credits
State child health insurance
Temporary Assistance for Needy Families (TANF)

Community Agencies
Churches
Crisis centers and hotlines
Family physician and pediatrician
Food banks
Health department
Hospital social service departments
Human resources offices
Mental-health clinics
Parent support groups for designated disabilities
Resource and referral agencies for child care
School district
Social security office

Contact information for these agencies can be found in the city/county/state/ government listing section of the local telephone book as well as through interagency and network telephone lists and communications systems.

have seen, a condition of ethical practice (NAEYC, 2005). Documentation, along with the formation of family partnerships, sets the stage for effective advocacy. "Early childhood educators are expected to be able to recognize high-risk or danger signals of disabling conditions" (Cook, Klein, & Tessier, 2008, p. 83). When delays or impairments are suspected, teachers must advocate for further screening by working in partnership with the child's family, connecting them to community agencies that provide screening, assessment, intervention, or educational services and assisting them in any way necessary.

It is certainly difficult to approach parents with information that there may be a problem regarding a child's health or development, but doing so is absolutely essential to the future well-being of both the child and the family. In many cases, parents may already suspect problems but not be able to articulate their concern, or they may fear the worst and this fear may prevent them from confronting the issue on their own. Sharing your concerns with parents and linking them to the resources that will provide further information and assistance may actually provide relief for them. Guidelines for conducting conferences and making referrals will be presented later in this chapter.

Disabling Condition of a Family Member

Finding out that someone has a disabling or handicapping condition or a chronic illness can be a traumatic event and send a family into crisis. "A family's response to a crisis depends on (a) the stressor event itself, (b) the resources that the family has for coping with the stressor, and (c) the specific meaning the family gives to the event" (Wright et al., 2007, pp. 144–145). Upon receiving the news, adults in the family will first be in shock and then inundated with information that might be vague and contain language that is new to them. They may be overwhelmed by the bureaucracy that surrounds services they need access to. Often, families dealing with such trauma isolate themselves or at least feel isolated from friends and family (Cook et al., 2008; Wright & Wright, 2006). This family trauma will affect a child even if the child is not the one diagnosed with the disabling condition. As an early childhood professional, you may be drawn into advocacy activities when a child you work with or the family member of a child you work with is identified with a handicapping condition.

Since 1968, congress has, through the efforts of many advocacy groups, passed laws that provide support for children and families of children with disabilities. In 1990, the **Individuals with Disabilities Education Act (IDEA)** was passed by congress, ensuring comprehensive early intervention services to young children and their families. IDEA clearly states that the role of the school is to support families before, during, and after identification is made. Public school systems are mandated to have procedures for defining and delivering educational services to identified children and families. Private and parochial schools and child care programs may or may not have extensive procedures in place and may rely exclusively on more community agencies to provide services. A full accounting of the law and what is required of programs is beyond the scope of this book. Our purpose here is to highlight the early childhood professional's role as an advocate for the family, that is, to stand ready to support the family in locating information and accessing services needed.

Advocating for Siblings

Siblings of children with disabling conditions may need the support of an advocate when they demonstrate the following characteristics through their conversation, play, or art work:

- Believe they caused the handicapping condition
- Feel they need to compensate for the child with a handicapping condition, that is—be the perfect child in the family
- Worry that they might "catch" the condition
- Encounter others who bully or ridicule them or their sibling
- Display jealousy of the attention family members are giving the identified child
- Take on, or are given, responsibilities beyond their age (Moore, Howard & McLaughlin, 2002).

Adult family members may or may not be aware of the impact of having a sibling with a disability has on other children in the family. If they are aware, they may feel overwhelmed by other responsibilities or just at a loss as to how to help the other children in the family. The early childhood professional can advocate for these children by sharing information with the family about changes in the siblings' demeanor or affect, providing parents with specific information about how to talk to children about disabilities, or, connecting them to sibling support groups that are active in the community. Such support groups can be located by contacting the local chapter of the Council of Exceptional Children (CEC) or their national Web site.

Suspicion of Child Abuse or Neglect

Child abuse consists of any act, or failure to act, which endangers a child's physical or emotional health and development (HelpGuide.org, 2007). Incidences of abuse and neglect have the potential to create both long- and short-term physical, psychological, and behavioral consequences for the child (Karr-Morse & Wiley, 1997). These consequences may include poor general health, low self-esteem, cognitive delays, relationship difficulties, depression or anxiety, substance abuse, eating disorders, spousal and child abuse, physical injury or death (Child Welfare Information Gateway, 2006; HelpGuide.org).

Not all abused or neglected children will suffer long-term consequences. Research has found a number of **protective factors** that contribute to a child's **resilience,** that is, his or her ability to cope following negative experiences. These factors include the child's age and developmental status when the abuse or neglect occurred, the type of abuse, its frequency, duration, and severity, and the relationship between the victim and his or her abuser (Chalk, Gibbons, & Scarupa, 2002). Other factors that foster a sense of resilience include availability of social support within the community and the presence of a caring adult in the child's life (Thomlison, 1997). Early childhood professionals are **mandated reporters** who serve as advocates to all children by being vigilant to the early warning signs of abuse and neglect and reporting their suspicions to the appropriate authorities, thereby initiating a process that ultimately affects the child in a positive way (NAEYC, 1996, 2003).

Michael Newman/PhotoEdit Inc.

Early childhood professionals are mandated reporters; that is, they are required by law to report suspected abuse or neglect.

Detecting Early Signs of Child Abuse

The first step in advocating for children who may be victims of child abuse or neglect is to recognize the symptoms. There are four general types of abuse: physical abuse, neglect, sexual abuse, and emotional maltreatment, but it is common for one child to experience more than one kind of abuse. For example, a child may be physically abused and neglected at the same time (Prevent Child Abuse America, 2007). Figure 3.5 provides definitions and common symptoms for the different types of abuse. Note that one symptom in isolation does not necessarily indicate abuse. What early childhood professionals should look for is a cluster of symptoms.

Causes of Child Abuse and Neglect

Child abuse and neglect happen at all levels of society. The causes of child abuse or neglect are varied and complex. It is not always deliberate or intentional. There are several factors in someone's life that may lead him or her to be abusive. Stress is one such factor. This stress can be induced by economic factors, unemployment, the illness or death of a family member, or isolation, divorce, or separation from domestic partners. Other factors that might lead someone to be abusive include

- physical or mental health problems
- difficulty controlling anger
- alcohol or drug abuse
- personal history of being abused (de Benedictis, Jaffe, & Segal, 2007; HelpGuide.org, 2007).

The best defense against child abuse and neglect is prevention. In addition to recognizing the signs of abuse, early childhood educators should be aware of factors that contribute to or cause abuse or neglect so they can support families who might be experiencing high-stress situations.

Reporting Suspected Abuse or Neglect

Although often uncomfortable, reporting documented suspected abuse is not only an act of advocacy for the child who cannot speak up for him- or herself, it is the law. The Child Abuse Prevention and Treatment Act (CAPTA), originally passed in 1974, mandates the reporting of suspected child abuse and neglect and, since 1996, all 50 states have enacted related

Figure 3.5 Definitions and Signs of Child Abuse

Physical Abuse: An injury resulting from physical aggression such as beating, hitting, pushing, shaking, pinching, or severe physical punishment. Even when injury is not intentional, the act is still considered abuse. Signs include:
- unexplained burns, bite marks, cuts, bruises, or welts in the shape of an object,
- antisocial behavior,
- resistance to going home, and
- fear of adults.

Sexual Abuse: Any sexual act between an adult and a child including penetration, fondling, violation of bodily privacy, intercourse, rape, commercial exploitation, or exposing children to adult sexuality. Signs include:
- inappropriate interest or knowledge of sexual acts,
- seductiveness,
- nightmares and bed-wetting,
- dramatic changes in appetite,
- avoidance of things related to sexuality, or rejection of own genitals or body,
- either overcompliance or excessive aggression, and
- fear of a particular person.

Emotional Abuse: Any attitude, behavior, or failure to act that interferes with a child's mental or social development including yelling, screaming, threatening, bullying, shaming, ignoring, exposure to violence, child exploitation, or abduction. Emotional abuse often exists alongside other forms of abuse. Signs include:
- shows extremes in behavior: overly compliant, demanding, passive, aggressive,
- apathetic,
- depressed,
- hostile,
- is either inappropriately adult-like or child-like,
- stressed,
- has difficulty concentrating, and
- eating disorders.

Neglect: A pattern of failure to provide for a child's basic needs. Three types of neglect have been identified:

Physical Neglect: Failure to provide food, clothing appropriate for the weather, supervision, a home that is clean and safe, and/or medical care, as needed.

Educational Neglect: Failure to enroll a school-aged child in school or provide necessary special education. This includes allowing excessive absenteeism.

Emotional Neglect: Failure to provide emotional support, love and affection. Signs of neglect include:
- unsuitable clothing for the weather,
- is frequently absent from school,
- consistently dirty and has severe body odor,
- extreme hunger,
- begs or steals food or money from classmates or teacher, and
- apparent lack of supervision: states there is no one home to provide care.

Source: HelpGuide.org, 2007; Child Help, 2007; Prevent Child Abuse America, 2007.

reporting laws. CAPTA also requires that states have legislation that provides immunity from prosecution for individuals who report suspected abuse in good faith.

> In most states persons who report suspected child abuse "in good faith" are absolutely immune from criminal and civil liability. For that reason, most health care attorneys advise a client that it is far better, in theory, to be faced with defending a civil action for reporting suspected abuse rather than the bleak alternative of defending action, if a child is injured or killed as a result of failing to make a report of suspected child abuse. (Smith, 2006)

Any individual who works with young children is a mandated reporter and is legally bound to report suspected child abuse or neglect. The extent of the knowledge necessary to elicit reporting varies from state to state. Some states require *reasonable cause to believe*; others stipulate *to know or suspect*. In either case, failure to report suspected child abuse can result in criminal or civil liability. In many states, early childhood professionals are mandated reporters not only if they suspect abuse or neglect but also if abuse or neglect is reported to them. For example, if a parent confides in you that a spouse has abused a child, you are then legally bound to report this to the proper authorities. To learn more about the specific statutes that govern mandatory reporting in your state, link to the Child Welfare Information Gateway and search for State Statutes' mandatory reporting page at www.childwelfare.gov/systemwide/laws_policies/state. The state statutes' page contains information for reporting issues for all 50 states.

Reports can be made to your community child protection agency, whose number you can find in your local phone book. There is also a National Abuse Hotline, 1-800-4-A-CHILD and each state has its own hotline number. If abuse is observed that is life-threatening, do not hesitate, call 911.

CONFERENCING AND REFERRALS

When you have well-documented concerns about a child's health, development, or well-being, sharing these with the family will lead to positive outcomes for all. The hardest part may be finding the right way to begin the conversation. When conferring with family members about issues related to their child's well-being, the following strategies and techniques will be helpful.

Be organized and well prepared

- Document your concerns through multiple observations done in different settings and over a time span of a 2- to 4-week period.
- Organize this documentation so that you can provide family members with specific examples, not generalized statements.
- Plan your presentation carefully and role-play the conference with a colleague (Gonzalez-Mena, 2007).

Scott Cunningham/Merrill

Developing partnerships with families is an important aspect of effective advocacy.

■ Anticipate that you might be met with resistance and even anger. You are going to be telling parents things they will not want to hear and many will not be able to accept this information immediately.

■ Have your referral strategy worked out. Be prepared to give parents specific names and phone numbers to call. Have brochures describing the services available. Offer assistance in making initial calls to agencies.

Pick the right time and place for the meeting

■ Ask family members to meet with you to discuss ways that you can help their child.

■ Let the parents know that they are welcome to bring other adult family members to the conference.

■ Schedule the meeting to assure that all attending have plenty of time to focus on the issues at hand. You will need to be ready to deal with emotions.

■ Provide child care away from where the meeting is to take place. Perhaps another teacher can watch the child and the child's siblings while you meet with the parents.

■ Ensure privacy for your meeting.

Open the meeting by restating your purpose: to help me, the early childhood professional, help your child

■ Ask family members how they feel their child is doing in school or in the program. By asking open-ended questions you give them a chance to express their observations, questions, or concerns. For example, if your concerns are about the child's social development, ask, "What kinds of activities does Amanda enjoy when she is with other children?" It could be that parents already sense a problem but do not know how to articulate it.

■ Listen carefully to what they are saying and try to link your concerns to theirs. By sharing your concern, you may validate a feeling the parent has, is afraid of, or is unable to express. Surprisingly, this often brings the parent a sense of relief.

Express your concerns clearly

■ Talk about specific behaviors, using anecdotes from your observations to illustrate your concerns.

■ Do not use jargon, labels, or acronyms.

■ Don't compare the child to other children but do draw comparisons with developmental guidelines. "Children this age are usually talking in complete sentences, but Robert is using noun-verb phrases."

- Provide appropriate material, such as developmental checklists or information about suspected conditions. Family members will need time and more information before they can come to grips with the situation.

Give a positive message about early detection or intervention

- Reassure the parent that at this point, we do not know if there is an issue or problem, but further screening will let us know exactly what we are dealing with and how best to handle it.
- Explain the referral process and what your expected outcome is. For example, if you are referring Sandra for language screening, let her parents know how, when, and where the screening will be done, by whom, and what information they expect.
- Explain the screening process by comparing it to noticing the first signs of the flu and going to the doctor for confirmation and medication. Not seeking and receiving timely medical intervention may make the illness worse. "Parents, especially, need support and encouragement to realize that screening is only a preliminary step and does not determine the definite existence of a disabling condition" (Cook et al., 2008, p. 83).
- Be empathetic, open, and available. Accept the family member's frustration, fear, or even anger as part of the process of the referral, not as a personal attack on you.

Refer family members to the appropriate person or agency

- Convey exactly what the next steps are.
- Have the appropriate referral numbers ready to give to the family. Explain exactly how to make the referral.
- If you feel it is appropriate, offer to make the call yourself.
- Except in the case of expected abuse or neglect, respect the family's need to wait, read more, and study the situation before acting. Parents may experience grief and disbelief when confronted with news about possible developmental delays. They certainly will encounter fear. All of these will create barriers to action. Remember, families will need time to process the information.

Follow up the conference with a phone call or second conference

- Ask the parents if they have any further questions.
- Continue to observe the child and document developmental movement or lack of developmental movement. It is important to proceed with confidence and sensitivity—but acting in the child's best interest. Be quietly persistent.

(The above strategies and techniques were compiled and adapted from the following sources: Cook et al., 2008; FirstSigns.org, 2007; Gonzalez-Mena, 2007; Wright et al., 2007; Wright & Wright, 2006.)

SUPPORTING FAMILY MEMBERS TO ADVOCATE FOR THEIR CHILD

Certainly, children with special needs and children who have lived in abusive situations will benefit greatly from parents and family members who are empowered to advocate for their best interest, but essentially one of the greatest assets any child can have is a family that is empowered to help itself. That is, a family that can advocate for each of their children's needs as well as their own. Early childhood professionals are in a position to help families develop their skills as advocates by first providing a model of effective advocacy and then by helping them translate their dreams for their children into action plans. Gonzalez-Mena (2007) suggests that asking parents to talk about their dreams for their children, not just their goals, stimulates their ability to actualize those dreams. The early childhood professional can then support the development of self-advocacy skills through conferences, newsletters, and workshops. Important self-advocacy skills include

- organizing information about their child,
- formulating and asking questions about their child's learning and development,
- seeking information from a wide range of sources,
- understanding federal and state laws that affect families and services to families,
- identifying characteristics of quality schools,
- networking with other families to share information and create communities that support all families, and most importantly, and
- maintaining their own health and their relationships with others (Wright & Wright, 2006).

Community agencies may provide support groups or advocacy training to families. As families learn to advocate for issues that are important to their children, they will be able to let their voices be heard for broader issues important to all children and families across the community, nation, and globe.

SUMMARY

Early childhood professionals are among the first to work with children and families over a sustained period of time and therefore are in a unique position to observe early signs of developmental delays or family stressors that might have a negative impact on the child's development and learning. Therefore, they have an ethical responsibility to recognize and document signs, consult with families and refer them to appropriate agencies, and support families who are in need of, or are receiving help. Finally, early childhood professionals should support parents and other family members to become advocates for themselves and their families.

RELEVANT CONCEPTS

federal poverty level

low-income families

Individuals with Disabilities Education Act (IDEA)

child abuse

protective factors

resilience

mandated reporters

FOR FURTHER READING

Child Poverty in America Today by Barbara Arright and David Maume (Eds.), 2007. Published by Greenwood Publishing Group.

What Money Can't Buy: Family Income and Children's Life Chances by Susan Mayer, 1998. Published by Harvard University Press.

Understanding Child Abuse and Neglect by Cynthia Crosson-Tower, 2007. Published by Allyn & Bacon.

Parents as Partners in Education: Families and Schools Working Together, 7th Edition, by Eugenia Hepworth Berger, 2008. Published by Merrill/Prentice Hall.

The Complete IEP Guide: How to Advocate for Your Special Ed Child, 4th Edition, by Lawrence M. Siegel, 2005. Published by Nolo.

LINKS TO ADVOCACY RESOURCES

Wrightslaw Yellow Pages for Kids

www.yellowpagesforkids.com

Use this site to find educational consultants, psychologists, educational diagnosticians, health care providers, academic therapists, tutors, speech language therapists, occupational therapists, coaches, advocates, and attorneys for children with disabilities.

Council for Exceptional Children

www.cec.sped.org

The Council for Exceptional Children (CEC) is the largest international professional organization dedicated to improving educational outcome for individuals with exceptionalities, students with disabilities, and/or the gifted.

IDEA

www.nichcy.org/idea.htm

This site provides resources related to IDEA and its implementing regulations.

QUESTIONS FOR REFLECTION AND DISCUSSION

1. Shannon is a 3-year-old child who has been in your program for about one year. Until recently he was even tempered and played well with other children. In the last week you have noticed a change in his temperament: He cries frequently, is angered easily, and has little interest in playing with others or engaging in normal classroom activities. Describe possible causes for this change in behavior and outline a course of action you could follow to learn more and get appropriate help for Shannon.

2. In this chapter, we have talked specifically about advocacy activities with individual children and families, but advocacy does not happen in isolation from community, state, and federal policies and regulations. Discuss the relationship between advocating for individuals you know and advocating for public policies that support the well-being of individuals you do not know.

3. Review the statutes related to reporting abuse or neglect in your state. Create a scenario that provides an example of when and how you, as an early childhood professional, would report suspected abuse or neglect.

ADVOCACY IN ACTION: APPLICATION ACTIVITIES

1. Using the local phone book and the Internet, create a referral list for your community.

2. Using the Internet, find information related to developmental milestones and red flags that would be helpful to use when observing children. Create a reference folder for future use.

3. Visit a local United Way agency and interview the director. Find out what services are available and how referrals are made and handled.

4. Interview the director of a child care program about the protocol and procedures used to refer families for services and to report suspected child abuse.

Chapter 4: Advocacy for Our Profession, Programs, and in the Private Sector

CONNECTIONS

When you finish school, how will you maintain your currency in the field? How will you effect needed changes in the programs you work in? What connections do you see between the welfare of children and families and the business community?

Profile of an Advocate

Lee Chen is a teacher in an inclusive state-funded pre-kindergarten housed in a public school in Anchorage, Alaska. Ms. Chen is a member of the Council for Exceptional Children (CEC), Division of Early Childhood (DEC), the International Reading Association (IRA), and the National Association for the Education of Young Children (NAEYC). She looks forward to receiving publications from these organizations and makes it a point to read each thoroughly and share them with colleagues. Through the journals and the associations' Web sites, Ms. Chen maintains currency in her field and often joins campaigns that foster respect for her profession as well as the well-being of children and families across the nation and in the global community.

There is a state affiliate of NAEYC in Anchorage and Ms. Chen serves as secretary. She also serves on the Professional Recognition Committee, which plans events and campaigns, including *The Week of the Young Child* that showcases the importance of the early years and fosters recognition and respect for the work of early childhood professionals. She regularly attends, and often presents at, state and local conferences. She has attended the international conference of DEC twice and is looking forward to making a presentation at the next one.

Ms. Chen uses the ideas she gains from reading professional journals and networking with her colleagues to foster changes within her school that reflect best practices. Under her leadership, her school has just implemented a curriculum based on the theme of social justice that fosters conflict resolution skills among children across multiple grade levels. In order to institute this change, teachers studied different models, developed a model that fit the unique needs of their student population, and worked with the principal to revise policies that were preventing consistent cross grade–level interactions. Ms. Chen and her committee were also successful in developing partnerships with local businesses to increase the number of volunteers working directly with children and providing necessary resources to implement the program.

A committee is now working with another district school to develop and implement a similar curricular design. The committee will be presenting a proposal to the school board to request a grant to assess the effectiveness of this curriculum as it relates to cognitive and social development as well as classroom management. Through advocacy efforts for her profession and program as well as advocacy within the private sector, Ms. Chen is affecting positive changes for the children and families she knows, and many she does not know.

Advocates like Ms. Chen, who work within their profession to strengthen its visibility, within their programs to foster best practice, and with business leaders in the private sector to develop policies and products that support growth, development, and learning can make significant contributions to the welfare of infants, young children, and their families. These advocacy efforts are often reflective in nature, interrelated, and incorporated seamlessly into other job responsibilities. But these contributions resonate not only in the advocate's own community but throughout the state, nation, and even global arena. The focus of this chapter is to describe advocacy strategies that showcase the profession, foster best practices within and across programs, and engage the private sector in ways that support the welfare of children and families. Skills needed to implement these strategies will be discussed in detail in Part II of this book.

ADVOCACY FOR THE PROFESSION

In Chapter 2, we stated that advocacy for the profession involves showcasing the field of early childhood in such a way that the public better understands and values the important work that early childhood professionals engage in every day. This effort is essential because, generally speaking, the field of early childhood, particularly in the area of child care and education, has low status and workers are undercompensated. In addition, advocacy efforts that give high visibility to quality programs increase the public's awareness of what quality care and education looks like, sounds like, and feels like to infants, children, and families. This awareness will not only promote the establishment of more high-quality programs but also the improvement of existing programs.

Maintaining a high visibility and respect for the profession through advocacy is necessary to increase public funding for research related to child development and effective practice and to fully fund programs for underserved populations. It is important to understand that although quality federal and state funded early childhood programs, such as Head Start, exist they are rarely funded at the level needed to serve the number of children and families that are eligible. It is a matter of equity; all children and families should have access to the resources needed in the formative years.

As mentioned in Chapter 2, self-advocacy—getting the knowledge, skills, and resources you need to do the best job you can with children and families—is an important component of advocating for the profession. By increasing your resources and developing your skills through grants, further education, or training you not only become better able to deliver care and education of the highest quality, but demonstrate your commitment to the field. This, in turn, increases the status of the profession in the eyes of the public.

Advocacy Strategies

There are many strategies early childhood professionals can use to advocate for the profession. A description of some follows.

Join Professional Organizations

Meeting with others to exchange ideas, whether in person, through readings, or virtually through Web site structures such as listservs and blogs, not only increases your knowledge base but also allows you to share your passion for your professions with others who are equally passionate. This helps combat the isolation that teachers often feel and fosters confidence in yourself and your pride in your profession. There are many professional organizations designed to meet the needs of early childhood professionals. Figure 4.1 provides Web site information for some of these organizations.

Figure 4.1 Early Childhood Professional Organizations

Association for Childhood Education International
www.acei.org

Council for Exceptional Children
www.cec.sped.org

Division of Early Childhood
www.dec.sped.org

First Class Teachers
www.firstclassteachers.org

International Reading Association
www.reading.org

National Association for the Education of Young Children
www.naeyc.org

National Association for Family Child Care
www.nafcc.org

National Council of Teachers of Mathematics
www.nctm.org

National Head Start Association
www.nhsa.org

Serve in Leadership Positions

All professional organizations have a governing structure that operates at the national or international level and often at the state and regional level. This structure provides multiple opportunities for early childhood professionals to develop and use leadership skills while working to support the profession. Examples of service to professional organizations include

1. Holding an office.
2. Serving on one or more committees. The committee structure of each organization will be different but most groups have a committee for membership, publication, event planning, policy development, publicity, and advocacy.
3. Writing or reviewing articles for publication.
4. Presenting at local, state, national, or international conferences.

Participate in Campaigns

Professional organizations often sponsor **campaigns** to bring attention to specific issues, raise awareness, or to define actions that need to be taken by elected officials. Campaigns often foster alliances among other organizations, thereby strengthening their voice in the political arena.

The **Worthy Wage Campaign** was a grassroots effort led by child care teachers, family child care providers, school age teaching staff, Head Start teachers and others who work directly with children. It ran from 1991 to 1996 and was coordinated by the Center for the Child Care Workforce, a division of American Federation of Teachers Educational Foundation (www.ccw.org). Its purpose was to mobilize efforts to improve compensation and work environments for the early care and education workforce. One of the main strategies used was to sponsor *Worthy Wage Day* on May 1 of each year. Community organizations and child care and education programs designed and implemented events that brought the media's and the public's attention to the need to improve conditions and compensation for child care workers. Even though the campaign is over, many communities continue to celebrate *Worthy Wage Day*.

Examples of other campaigns include *The Week of the Young Child* sponsored by NAEYC and *The Week of the Classroom Teacher* sponsored by ACEI. Organizations often sponsor letter-writing campaigns aimed at letting legislators know the position of the early childhood community on crucial policy and funding legislation. To find out about current campaigns, check the journals and Web sites of different professional organizations.

Serve as a Community Resource

Early childhood professionals can represent their profession through service on community planning committees or by speaking to philanthropic organizations, such as the Shriners, about the needs of children and families. Serving as an elected official, such as on a school board or on the city council also showcases the profession and brings an important perspective to the table. Another way to advocate for the profession within the community is to speak at public meetings about the critical need for high-quality care and education and family services. Still another way is to write press releases, essays, or letters to the editor for publication in the local media.

Community events showcase the importance of the field of early care and education while developing partnerships within the community and among families.

Testify at Public Hearings

Early childhood professionals, because of their training and experience, have an expertise that needs to be present when public policies or pending legislation that concerns children and families is formulated or discussed. It is the early childhood advocate's responsibility to keep the needs of infants, children, and families at the forefront of these important decisions.

ADVOCACY WITHIN INDIVIDUAL PROGRAMS

Early childhood professionals often find themselves in the position of advocating for changes within their programs or schools to foster the use of best practices in early care and education. Changes needed may be specific, such as developing a school lunch schedule that provides early childhood classrooms large blocks of time needed to engage children in meaningful exploratory and discovery activities. Or, desired changes may be more general in nature, such as the implementation of a school-wide anti-bias curriculum.

Changes are easy to implement if they do not involve other professionals, need additional resources, or are impacted by existing policies. For example, after attending a workshop at a state conference for early education, a third-grade teacher understands that he needs to broaden the scope of initiative and choice-making opportunities available to his students. He feels the best way to do this is to create a center system where children choose from multiple activities designed to fulfill the same learning goal. Because he works in a self-contained classroom, he is able to make the changes needed without extensive advocacy efforts. However, a teacher from another school, who attended the same workshop, wants to make similar changes but encounters problems with resources, the belief system of the principal and two of the other four third-grade teachers, and with the school's schedule. This teacher needs to advocate for change by working with her colleagues, her administrator, and the school business partners. Steps for developing a plan for and carrying out steps of advocacy will be discussed further in Chapters 6, 7, and 8. Figure 4.2 provides examples of conditions within a program that require advocacy.

Figure 4.2 Issues That Require Advocacy

If, based on your knowledge and experience, you believe your program should apply for national accreditation.

If, based on your knowledge and experience, you believe the assessment system used in your school or program is not developmentally appropriate.

If, based on your knowledge and experience, you believe that there needs to be more continuity of care and education across programs in your community or grade levels in your school.

If, based on your knowledge and experience, you believe that the mandated curriculum you are required to teach does not actively engage children.

If, based on your knowledge and experience, you believe the program you work in needs to implement more family-friendly policies.

If, based on your knowledge and experience, you believe there needs to be a stronger focus on the arts in your program or school.

If, based on your knowledge and experience, you believe that the program or school you work at needs to become inclusive.

If, based on your knowledge and experience, you believe that the food program for your school or center does not offer nutritional choices to children.

If, based on your knowledge and experience, the policies for admission to your program or school are biased in any way.

Another way to decide whether or not advocating for a change in the curriculum of your school or program is necessary is to look at practices that have been deemed developmentally inappropriate. These practices include:

- Highly linear instruction, especially when it follows a linear timetable
- Heavy reliance on whole group instruction
- Fragmented lessons without connections that are meaningful to children
- Rigid adherence to a packaged "one-size-fits-all" curriculum
- Teachers following a predetermined script without regard to children's response
- Highly prescriptive requirements, along with rigid timetable for achieving them
- Narrow focus (for example, only on literacy and math instruction) (Copple & Bredekamp, 2008, p. 54)

The first step in advocating for program or curriculum change is always to work with the program administrator, building principal, assistant principal, curriculum coordinator, school counselor, and grade-level committees. But sometimes the changes you feel are needed relate to school district policies. When this is the case, and you work in a public school system, you will need to work with the local school board or the board of trustees to advocate for needed changes. What follows here is a discussion of how school boards operate.

Responsibilities of School Boards

Running a public school district is a difficult and complex endeavor and is the charge of a locally elected school board. As representatives of their community, board members set a unified mission and vision by adopting goals and standards and monitoring progress toward these goals, thus ensuring accountability across all schools. School boards oversee all facets of the district including hiring and firing personnel, contracting services for such things as transportation, meals, and maintenance, and establishing practices related to curriculum and assessment. In this capacity, they create and oversee the implementation of many policies.

In most districts, school board members are elected and represent different geographical zones in the community. However, in a small but growing percent of urban areas, school boards are politically appointed by mayors. Also, because of state and national accountability systems, low-performing schools or school districts may be run by state education agencies or other entities. Nonetheless, school board members are dedicated volunteers who represent a wide variety of backgrounds and experience in education. As a body, they have a great deal of responsibility because their work has tremendous impact on both the quality of education and the local tax base.

Most school boards are comprised of five to eight members each elected for a four-year term of office. However, many board members serve multiple terms. They meet monthly in a public session but may meet more often in private to conduct business related to personnel decisions. All other business of the board is conducted in full view of the public. Agendas are usually published 24 hours before the meeting. Meetings are often broadcast live on public television or radio stations. It is important to note that even though the meetings and work of the board is to be conducted in public, these are not public meetings where anyone can stand and be recognized. However, individuals can request to speak at an upcoming meeting by contacting the superintendent's office and asking to be placed on the agenda.

Advocates' Responsibility to the Board

Given the complexity of the responsibilities of being a board member and the reality that these elected officials may not all have training in education, specifically early childhood education, it becomes the job of early childhood professionals to be proactive and provide current and accurate information to the board as it relates to policies affecting young children and families.

You will find it easier to work with the school board if you have attended meetings and are acquainted with the members that represent your school and your neighborhood, if you live in the district. Personal relationships are important, and understanding each school board member's perspective can help facilitate reaching your objective. Specific tactics for effective advocacy will be presented in Chapters 6, 7, and 8. However, here are some general guidelines to keep in mind when working with school boards:

Early childhood professionals often promote the well-being of children and families by speaking at public functions such as school board meetings.

- Always make your building principal aware of your advocacy goals and plans to work with the school board.
- Talk to board members individually before you develop an advocacy plan. Find out where they stand and what information would help them understand your position on an issue.
- Get all of the facts before you plan your tactics. If your issue concerns a new curriculum, read that curriculum thoroughly and find its research and theoretical base. If the issue concerns a policy that you feel jeopardizes young children and their families in some way, get a copy of the policy and study it carefully.
- Form coalitions with parents and teachers from other schools and from members of the community to demonstrate district-wide support for your issue.
- Provide information that is tailored to the needs of the school board membership. Prepare it carefully and make it jargon free and easy to read.
- Demonstrate the economic feasibility of the program or policy you are supporting as well as its educational value.
- Maintain your composure when speaking. Remain courteous, courageous, and hopeful.
- Be persistent. **Systemic change** takes time.

ADVOCACY IN THE PRIVATE SECTOR

Small businesses and large corporations operating in the **private sector** of the American economy often have policies that positively or negatively affect children and families. For example, many large businesses subsidize child care for employees or grant employees leave time to volunteer at schools or community youth organizations. Others may not support families in any way. Also, some corporations create and/or market products in ways that negatively impact children. Private sector advocacy involves working with businesses and corporations to develop and implement products and policies that support the well-being of infants, toddlers, and young children. What follows is a discussion of three specific kinds of advocacy work that takes place within the private sector.

Developing Family-Friendly Policies

One form of advocacy in the private sector attempts to persuade policy makers to take an interest in and support the well-being of their employees and their families through the implementation of **family-friendly policies.** Examples of such policies include:

- Flextime: allowing family members flexible working hours so that they can attend conferences, programs, meetings, or participate as volunteers at their child's school.
- Child Care Benefits: taking part in tax-benefit programs offered by state and federal governments to offset the cost of child care for working families.
- On-site Child Care: offering child care services at the business site. This is often feasible for large corporations such as hospitals, but not for smaller companies. However, they can often partner with nearby child care facilities and subsidize the facility in a way that benefits their employees.
- Family Leave Time: offering paid or unpaid leave benefits to employees that allow them time off to care for sick family members without jeopardizing their jobs.
- Maternity/Paternity Leave: providing paid leave to parents welcoming a new baby, adoptive child, or foster child into their family. The law already provides unpaid leave.
- Health Insurance: offering affordable medical and dental insurance to employees and their families.

Partnering with the Private Sector

A second form of advocacy in the private sector of the local economy is to work to develop partnerships between early childhood programs and area businesses. For example, Abeona House is a Reggio-inspired child care center located in a developing neighborhood/business district within a large city. The center joined the neighborhood business association and enjoys supportive partnerships with area merchants. One business provides a meeting room for family education activities and for board meetings. The association works together to resolve mutual issues that arise; for example, traffic flow, to ensure safety and convenience not only for the children and families of Abeona House, but also for patrons of all the area's businesses.

Schools often have business partners that support them not only through funds, but also through volunteer efforts. Avondale Industries is a large shipbuilding company located in Bridge City, Louisiana. The volunteer coordinator at Bridge City Elementary School contacted the personnel director at the company and asked for help implementing a reading program, STAIR (Start the Adventure in Reading). This program pairs volunteers with children in the second grade for 30-minute reading sessions each week. Eventually, policies were developed that provided any Avondale employee time during their workday to volunteer at the school. During one year, 96 Avondale employees volunteered as reading tutors. This program had a positive effect, not only for the children at Bridge City Elementary School, but for the entire community.

Campaigning for Fair Practices and Positive Products

There are many industries in the private sector of the economy that promote products that are either unsafe or detract from the positive mental growth and development of infants, toddlers, and young children. Examples include the tobacco and alcohol industries, food-product companies, music and video game industries, and toy manufacturers. In addition, advertising often targets young children and creates an environment that promotes consumerism among our most vulnerable citizens.

These industries are so large and so entrenched in our daily lives that we may become overwhelmed by the prospect of taking them on. They also seem distant because their operations are based throughout the world.

However, it is important to the healthy development of infants and young children that we advocate for family-friendly products, practices, and advertising. One way that individuals can make a positive difference in this arena is to join national campaigns sponsored by **nonprofit advocacy groups.**

The central mission of these nonprofit advocacy groups is to impact public thinking by providing information and proposing advocacy steps that will bring their campaigns to communities across the nation and world. These organizations exist to serve and promote the common good but, in doing so, they also create opportunities for individuals to engage in advocacy and become actively involved in civic life (Alvarado, 2003). Local advocates or advocacy groups can take the information provided by the nonprofit group via the internet and work at the community level to enlist support for positive practices. In fact, nonprofits rely heavily on community volunteers to provide the manpower and resources needed to be effective. The following are just a few examples of nonprofit advocacy groups that promote family friendly products, practices, and advertising.

■ Center for Screen-Time Awareness
www.tvturnoff.org

The Center for Screen-Time Awareness, formerly known as TV-Turnoff Network and TV-Free America, is a nonprofit organization that encourages children and adults to watch much less television. The organization takes the point of view that instead of waiting for others to make TV better, individuals can reclaim TV time and use it to promote positive interactions within families and communities. They work to raise public awareness concerning the negative impact of excessive television viewing.

The center sponsors *TV-Turnoff Week*. This is a grassroots project endorsed by 65 national organizations including the American Medical Association. The center's Web site provides material that local schools, clubs, and faith-based organizations can use to promote this annual event.

The center also sponsors a program called *More Reading, Less TV.* This is a four-week program that helps elementary teachers motivate their students to read more. Their Web site contains fact sheets, program information, a message board, and information on taking action.

■ **Campaign for Tobacco-Free Kids**

www.tobaccofreekids.org

This nonprofit advocacy group sponsors a site called E-Champions Action Center that provides information about state and federal initiatives to stop the tobacco industry from targeting children through their advertisements. Fact sheets are also available to use in local campaigns. Individuals can register to receive regular action alerts from the organization.

■ **Campaign for a Commercial-Free Childhood (CCFC)**

www.commercialexploitation.org

The Campaign for a Commercial-Free Childhood (formerly Stop Commercial Exploitation of Children) is a national coalition of health care professionals, educators, parents, and advocacy groups that seek to counter the harmful effects of marketing to children. CCFC sponsors conferences, congressional briefings, and grassroots efforts to build public awareness of the harms associated with commercialism. In 2003, this group was successful in getting the Golden Marble Awards, the advertising industry's celebration of marketing to children, cancelled. In 2008, CCFC was able to prevent the Disney Corporation from marketing Baby Einstein videos as educational products.

The Web site for this organization provides fact sheets and action tips as well as a PowerPoint outreach presentation on the harms of marketing to children.

■ **Teachers Resisting Unhealthy Children's Entertainment (TRUCE)**

www.truceteachers.org

TRUCE is an organization of early childhood professionals who work to promote a positive play environment for children by providing parents and community members with information about how children's entertainment and toys affect their behavior and learning. Their work is aimed at eliminating marketing aimed at exploiting children and reducing the sale of toys and entertainment that promotes violence. To that end, TRUCE produces and distributes written material, including guides to buying toys, flyers related to media violence, fact sheets related to the impact of violent toys, and articles about the importance of nonviolent imaginative play. This material is available on their Web site and they encourage you to print and distribute it.

■ **The Alliance for Childhood**
www.allianceforchildhood.org

The Alliance for Childhood promotes policies and practices that support children's healthy development, love of learning, and joy in living. The organization focuses on restoring child initiated imaginative play, disseminating information concerning the possible hazards in prolonged computer use by children, and bringing public attention to the health-related dangers of high-stakes testing. Fact sheets and suggestions for action are regularly posted on their website.

Major industries are regulated by public laws and commissions. For example, the U.S. Consumer Product Safety Commission is responsible for protecting the public from risks of serious injury or death from more that 15,000 types of consumer products under its jurisdiction. The Federal Communication Act of 1934 governs radio and television broadcasting and its policies are revisited regularly by congress. Campaigns that raise questions about the policies of corporations and industries will come to the attention of legislators. This emphasizes the important interrelationship between advocacy in the private sector and public policy advocacy, which will be discussed in Chapter 5.

SUMMARY

Advocates who work within their profession to strengthen its visibility, within their programs to foster best practice, and with business leaders in the private sector to develop policies and products that support growth, development, and learning can make significant contributions to the welfare of infants, young children, and their families.

Early childhood professionals can advocate for their profession by joining and serving in leadership roles in professional organizations, participating in campaigns that promote the profession, acting as a community resource, and testifying at public meeting about the needs of infant and toddlers, young children, and their families. Advocates must be alert to needed changes within their program or schools that will foster healthier environments for children and families.

Early childhood professionals should also work in the private sector to promote family friendly policies in the workplace and develop partnerships with local businesses that will enhance the care and education of young children. It is also important to maintain vigilance regarding the actions of major industries whose practices often affect the well-being of children through their products or advertisements. One way to do this is to join forces with nonprofit advocacy groups whose mission is to impact public thinking through national campaigns.

RELEVANT CONCEPTS

campaigns

Worthy Wage Campaign

systemic change

private sector

family-friendly policies

nonprofit advocacy groups

FOR FURTHER READING

Consumed: How Markets Corrupt Children, Infantilize Adults, Swallow Citizens Whole by Benjamin Barker, 2007. Published by W.W. Norton and Company.

Golden Legacy: How Golden Books Won Children's Hearts, Changed Publishing Forever and Became an American Icon Along the Way by Leonard S. Marcus, 2007. Published by Random House Children's Books.

Celebrating Young Children and Their Teachers: The Mimi Brodsky Chenfeld Reader, by Mimi Brodsky Chenfeld, 2006. Published by Redleaf Press.

Remote Control Childhood? Combating the Hazards of Media Culture by Diane L. Levin, 1998. Published by the National Association for the Education of Young Children.

Finding Our Way: The Future of American Early Care and Education by Moncrieff Cochran, 2007. Published by the National Association for the Education of Young Children.

LINKS TO ADVOCACY RESOURCES

U.S. Consumer Product Safety Commission

www.cpsc.gov

Provides information about product safety and regulations.

Federal Communications Commission

www.fcc.gov

Oversees the radio, television, wire, satellite, and cable industries. Contains legislative alerts to notify the public when important bills are coming up for vote by congress.

New American Dream

www.newdream.org

Provides information about marketing ads that target children and sponsors many campaigns aimed at positive consumerism.

Center for the Child Care Workforce

www.ccw.org

A network that provides timely information and analysis of relevant research, policy, and organizing efforts that support or impede improvements in early care and education employment conditions.

QUESTIONS FOR REFLECTION AND DISCUSSION

1. Discuss the importance of maintaining currency in the field of early childhood. What does it mean to be current? What is the relationship between being current and being an informed advocate?

2. Read about the Week of the Young Child on the NAEYC Web site (www.naeyc.org) and The Week of the Classroom Teacher on the ACEI Web site (www.acei.org). Compare the two campaigns by contrasting their purpose and their audience. Suggest effective events for each of the campaigns. How do these campaigns impact the profession?

3. Look through the local newspapers and cut out articles that outline issues related to young children and families. What seem to be the hot topics in your community? Who are the agencies or leaders responsible for implementing policies related to these topics? What is the public's role? What voice could the early childhood professional bring to these meetings?

4. Review the nonprofit Web sites listed in this chapter. Discuss the different activities used to advocate for change. Suggest other activities that you feel might be effective in your local community or among your friends and colleagues that would support the cause of the Web site.

ADVOCACY IN ACTION: APPLICATION ACTIVITIES

1. Attend a public hearing or school board meeting in your community. Reflect on how the meeting was conducted, who attended and what their roles were, and what issues were discussed that impacted children and families. Was an early childhood professional present at the meeting? How did (or how could) the voice of an early childhood professional affect the outcome of the meeting?

2. Working in groups of four, interview several early childhood professionals and discuss changes they feel need to happen in their programs. Ask them to discuss how they see their role in making positive change happen. What strategies do they know of or have they used. Compare the responses of the individuals interviewed. Of the individuals interviewed, whom do you identify with the most? Why?

3. Search the Web for advocacy groups that work to make the practices of industry more responsive to the needs of infants and young children. Reflect on what you could do to support this work in your local community.

Chapter 5: Political Activism

CONNECTIONS

What city, state, or federal policies directly influence your well-being? How are these policies formulated and enforced? How would you go about changing a policy that was negatively affecting the lives of children and families?

Profile of an Advocate

Shandra Wilson is the President and Chief Executive Officer of a statewide child advocacy network in the Gulf Coast Region of the United States. She founded this not-for-profit organization in 1990 to provide a voice for children and families. Before becoming politically active, Shandra worked as a kindergarten teacher, a child care center director, and an instructor at a community college. Through her work, she developed a valuable network consisting of contacts in the business world, community leaders who worked in family service agencies, and other early childhood professionals who were dedicated to making a difference for children. She also worked on a legislative committee charged with developing child care policies that would impact early care and education across the state.

As she gained more experience with the legislative process, Shandra found her political voice. She founded the advocacy network and began working with service providers, funding agents, legislators, and community leaders throughout the region. In her current position, she speaks to policy makers about the problems of real children and real families. She uses authentic stories, thereby connecting a *face* to the statistics that define problems like lack of health care or affordable high-quality child care. This makes the issues real to people who have been given the power and responsibility to effect positive change. She is always armed with strategic information and data necessary for the formulation or reform of policies affecting children and families.

Ms. Wilson leads a team of dedicated volunteer advocates. Together, they are impacting the region's children by working to expand health care coverage for uninsured children and pregnant women. They are also promoting legislation that mandates a quality rating system for child care licensing. Even though her busy schedule can sometime feel overwhelming, Shandra never loses sight of her main goal—to foster healthy environments for children and families.

An advocate is someone who stands up for the interest of others. When advocates identify problems, service gaps, injustices, and/or possible mistakes or unintended consequences of policies and procedures used by government agencies or private corporations, they work to find a solution. The right to attempt to influence public legislation and policy making is based on the First Amendment to the Constitution, which says that Congress shall make no law abridging the right of people *to petition the government for a redress of grievances.* You can help improve the education and well-being of children and families in your community by becoming involved in local, state, and federal policy making. Your participation as an educator will both raise the profile of the early childhood profession and also generate needed input and valuable ideas.

To effectively influence the creation, implementation, or regulation of **public policy,** you must know some basic facts about the legislative process and understand different strategies you can use to influence it. In this chapter we will review federal and state procedures as they relate to policy development.

TYPES OF POLICY ADVOCACY

"Public policies help define, in significant ways, the context in which large numbers of children and their families live" (Goffin & Lombardi, 1988, p. 8). Therefore, whether you are a parent, teacher, or caregiver, your expertise, training, and experience is critical to the process of developing public policies. The experience and perspective of those you advocate for is also vital to a policy's development. If legislators and civic leaders do not hear from their **constituents,** the people that they represent—the people that elected them, that there is a problem, they will not be aware of the needs of their communities. If no one tells them about the negative impact of pending or existing legislation or policies on their communities, they will not feel a need to do anything about it. The advocate's role in policy development is to inform public officials of the needs in the communities. When legislators and civic leaders understand how policies affect people's lives, they are better able to develop, revise, and/or fund projects that foster the well-being of their constituents.

Four basic types of policy advocacy have been identified: **case advocacy, administrative advocacy, legislative advocacy,** and **class advocacy.** Each operates at all levels of government—local, state, and federal. Each type shares the common focus of trying to change public systems to better serve children and families but differs in the target of their efforts. A brief description of each type of policy advocacy follows:

■ *Case Advocacy:* This type of advocacy involves efforts to secure appropriate services from a public agency for a particular child (Goffin & Lombardi, 1988). For example, an early interventionist acting on behalf of a family with a child with disabilities files a petition to secure Supplemental Security Income (SSI) to cover health expenses for the child.

■ *Administrative Advocacy:* Efforts are directed toward working with government agencies to develop appropriate regulations and guidelines for program implementation (Goffin & Lombardi, 1988). For example, a group of social workers lobby the government agency that oversees the foster care system in their community to develop a policy that limits the number of cases each worker is responsible for.

■ *Legislative Advocacy:* Advocates involved in this type of advocacy identify needed policies or evaluate existing or proposed policies to assure that current legislation protects and serves the best interests of children (Goffin & Lombardi, 1988). For example, a preschool teacher testifies before a legislative committee in support of a bill to limit the use of standardized testing of young children.

■ *Class Advocacy:* Here the focus is on the needs of a large group (a class) of children and frequently involves the judicial system; advocates work through litigation as agents of change on behalf of children (Goffin & Lombardi, 1988).

ROLES OF CITIZENS IN POLICY DEVELOPMENT

There are three basic roles an individual can assume to influence the development or implementation of public policy—that of expert, advocate, or community member (Decker & Decker, 2005). At one time or another, early childhood professionals will be called upon to fulfill all three roles. The **expert** reviews and evaluates the research literature pertinent to some issue, gives testimony at public hearings, creates brochures that outline the effects of policies, and assists public officials in understanding the effect of policies and legislation on the general public.

In the advocate's role, an individual works to promote, defend, or defeat policies and programs she believes are in the best interest of specific members of the community. An advocate takes a stand, spreads the word, and creates visibility for the issue. She uses the information provided by experts to develop campaigns to create, support, or change policies that impact children and families. Teachers and other early childhood professionals are in a unique position to understand the needs of children and families and also understand how legislation and policies affect them in both positive and negative ways and therefore are often called upon to act as advocates.

As members of the community, individuals influence policy making by being vocal, visible, and informed citizens who are vigilant regarding the accountability of government leaders and agencies. Community members can attend hearings and testify, telling their own stories, thus providing policy makers with knowledge of the effect of legislation and policies

Advocates often testify before congressional bodies regarding legislation that is important for the well-being of young children and families.

Stockbyte/Jupiter Images Picturequest – Royalty Free

on their constituents. Community members can also affect policy development by becoming informed voters and carefully studying the qualifications and positions of those running for election or reelection.

THE LEGISLATIVE PROCESS

No matter how one chooses to influence public policy, it is important for advocates to have a general understanding of the federal and state legislative process as they work to improve the lives of children and families. What follows is an overview of the federal legislative process as it relates to policy development. The makeup and operation of each state's legislative body is unique, but the process for policy development is similar to the federal process.

Branches of Government

There are three branches of government each charged with a different function. The legislative branch enacts laws while the executive branch has the responsibility to carry out these laws. The judicial branch of government interprets laws and resolves any conflicts between the other two branches. Therefore, even though bills are initiated and passed in the legislative branch of government, the executive and judicial branches play a significant role in the eventual implementation of legislation.

Legislative Branch

Congress, which consists of the Senate and the House of Representatives, is the federal legislative body. Every state has two U.S. senators and at least one representative. The number of representatives for each state is determined by that state's population. Congress meets in Washington, DC throughout the year. All states but Nebraska also have a legislative body that consists of two chambers, the Senate and the House of Representatives, or Assembly. Most state legislative bodies meet for a limited number of days each year. Some meet year round and a few meet only every other year. All legislators at both the federal and state level are elected officials. They are elected to represent the ideas and interests of their communities; therefore, the public has the right and the responsibility not only to *know* their elected officials' position on pending policy legislation but also to *communicate* their ideas, therefore influencing the way they are represented.

Federal legislation creates and influences many **funding streams** that affect local programs and services provided to young children and their families. For example, Head Start, the Child Care and Development Block Grant, and Title I of the Elementary and Secondary Education Act all developed from federal legislation and provide funds to states, school districts, and community agencies. There are three main categories of funding legislation: (1) authorizing bills, (2) reauthorizing bills, and (3) appropriation bills that oversee discretionary spending. **Authorizing bills** create programs, such as Head Start. These bills identify the grantee, the desired funding level, and other program requirements such as what kinds of services must be provided and to whom. Even though ideal funding levels are identified, the bill's authorization does not guarantee that those funding levels will be appropriated. Advocates for particular programs must become involved and lobby not only for the passage of the bill authorizing the program but also for funding the program at the optimal level.

Reauthorization bills are meant to renew existing programs. These bills provide the opportunity for the public to review the effectiveness of programs and make suggestions in procedures or funding levels. For example, the Reauthorization of Elementary and Secondary Act, originally passed in 1965, is now reauthorized every five years, providing advocates with opportunities to influence public policy during the review process.

Appropriation bills govern discretionary spending and are crafted and passed by committees separate from those that work on authorization legislation. These bills authorize direct spending on activities outlined in the program. Legislation directing discretionary appropriations to Head Start, child care, education, and other human service programs is passed every year. An important skill for advocates is to be able to locate and track legislation as it moves through the process of authorization. Many advocacy groups network to provide such information to local advocates and thereby maintain a high level of vigilance related to bills that affect, directly or indirectly, programs that serve children and families.

Executive Branch

The executive branch of government is responsible for regulating the laws passed by the legislative branch. They create the rules by which the laws are enforced. The federal executive branch of government consists of the president and vice president, 14 cabinet-level departments, 29 agencies, and 11 independent regulatory commissions. In most states, the legislative branch is headed by a governor and lieutenant governor and also contains cabinet-level departments. There may also be independent agencies, boards, or commissions that serve to regulate certain aspects of the government. Many officials that work within the executive branch, at the federal or state level, are elected by the public. If not elected, then these officials are appointed by those that are elected. This provides the public with significant power, in the form of votes, in the process of government.

Judicial Branch

The purpose of the judicial system is to ensure that policies do not violate the constitution of a state or of the United States. Therefore, proposed legislative requirements are subject to challenge and this challenge will be heard in the courts. The federal judiciary consists of the Supreme Court, the U.S. Court of Appeals, and the U.S. District Court. Federal judges are appointed by members of the executive branch and approved by members of the legislative branch of government. States also have trial courts and appellate courts, which are equivalent to the U.S. Supreme Court. Judges at the state level may be either elected or appointed as decided by state and local constitutions.

Understanding Your State and Local Government

The activities of state and local government agencies are regulated by the individual state's constitution and local bylaws and so will differ from one community to the next. To be an effective advocate, it is important to know the legislative rules and processes of your state as well as procedures for your municipality. Every government entity has a Web site that explains how it works and how its staff or elected officials can be contacted. One way to begin finding out about your own state government's structure is to use the National Conference of State Legislature's Web site, www.ncsl.org. This Web site provides a database of information about each state's legislative process and links to their home page. You will also be able to find a similar Web site that provides details about the procedures in your city or town.

HOW A BILL BECOMES A LAW

There are many steps involved in the development of legislation. Each step represents an opportunity for advocates to support or refute the merits of the proposal. The writers of the constitution intended for the process to be long and difficult and include multiple opportunities for citizen input. It is important to note that bills can change as they proceed along the path because committees add or delete provisions. It sometimes happens that an advocate can help in the development of a bill but end up opposing the bill because provisions were added or deleted that changed its effectiveness as perceived by those who originally proposed it. This points out the importance of **tracking legislation** so that individual advocates and advocacy groups can be aware of what is happening to the bill at any point in time and remain involved in maintaining the original integrity of the bill as it passes through the legislative process. What follows here is a brief review of each step.

Development and Introduction

The first step in creating a law is to develop the idea. Ideas come from many different sources, including the general public. Advocacy groups often work to develop ideas for programs or policies (legislation) that support children and families. As their ideas become more defined, they find a legislator to sponsor a bill that outlines the goals of the project. This legislator is called the **champion.**

The legislator and her staff will work together with an advocate or advocacy group to formulate the bill, and when it is ready, it is given a number and introduced in the legislative session by its sponsor. The numbering system for bills includes an indication of which legislative branch the bill was introduced in. H. R. signifies a House of Representatives bill; S. signifies a Senate bill. The bill is then ready to be referred to the appropriate committee for review.

Committee Referral

Committees are made up of small groups of senators or representatives and specialize in different areas such as foreign relations or agriculture. The revenue committee and the education committee often hear legislation that will directly impact children and families. When a bill reaches a committee, it is placed on the committee's calendar. It will be considered by a subcommittee or the committee as a whole. The bill is then carefully reviewed. Often public hearings are held to provide an opportunity to hear views from the executive branch, experts, other public officials, supporters, and opponents of the proposed legislation.

Floor Action

After the hearings are completed, the subcommittee meets to "mark up" the bill. They make changes and amendments before they recommend the bill to the full committee. If a subcommittee votes not to report legislation to the full committee, the bill dies. After receiving a subcommittee's report, the full committee either conducts further hearings or votes on the subcommittee's recommendations and reports its decision to the House or Senate. The committee chairperson then instructs staff to prepare a written report that includes the purpose of the bill, the position of the executive branch, views of dissenting members of the committee, the bill's impact on existing laws, budgetary considerations, and any new taxes or tax increases that will be required by the bill.

After the bill is reported back to the house of origin, it is placed on the legislative calendar for "floor action," or debate, before the full membership. Once the debate has ended and any amendments to the bill have been approved, the full membership will vote for or against the bill. Bills approved by one chamber of the Congress are sent to the other chamber where the bill follows generally the same route through committee and floor action.

Conferencing

The receiving chamber may approve the bill as received, reject it, ignore it, or change it. If only minor changes are made to a bill in the second chamber, it is common for it to go back to the origination chamber for concurrence. If the second chamber changes the bill significantly, a "conference committee" made up of members of both chambers will be formed to reconcile the differences. If this committee cannot agree, the bill simply dies. If the committee does agree on a compromise version of the bill, a conference report is prepared describing the committee's recommendations for change. Both chambers must approve of the conference report before it is sent to the president.

Executive Action

If the president approves of the legislation, he or she signs it and it becomes law. If the president takes no action on the bill for ten days while Congress is in session, the bill will automatically become law. The president can also choose to veto the bill outright or take no action on the bill for ten days after Congress has adjourned. If no action is taken after Congress has adjourned, the bill dies. This is known as a "pocket veto." When the president vetoes a bill, Congress may attempt to "override the veto" by calling for a roll call vote. Two-thirds of the members present in sufficient numbers for a quorum must approve the bill for it to become law.

The process of passing legislation at the federal level is similar but not always identical to the process used in state legislatures. To successfully track bills through the state legislative process and provide input at crucial times, it is necessary for advocates to become thoroughly familiar with the procedures in their own state.

Figure 5.1 provides a quick overview of the path from idea to legislation.

INFLUENCING POLICY DECISIONS

There are many ways to influence policy decisions at every level of government. "You don't have to be an expert to make a difference, and you don't have to go to Washington, DC or your state Capitol to lobby. Good advocates make opportunities wherever they go" (Amidei, 2002, p. 14). Understanding the policy making process is the first step in effective advocacy. The next step is to understand how you can influence this process.

Influencing the Legislative Branch

Advocates can influence the legislative branch of government in many ways. For example they can:

- Suggest ideas for programs and policies (laws) that will positively affect children and families.
- Draft policies and enlist legislators to sponsor or cosponsor legislation.
- Educate the public about the needs of such policies or the negative effect of existing policies, via grass roots advocacy campaigns.
- Communicate with elected officials through e-mails, letters, phone calls, and visits.

Figure 5.1 The Path from Idea to Law

1. An idea is developed and citizen support is generated.
2. A Congressional sponsor for the bill is chosen. It is best to have sponsors in both chambers of congress.
3. The Congressional sponsor, or champion, introduces the bill and it is given an identification number.
4. The bill is referred to one or more committees.
5. Committee hearings are held to discuss the bill in a public forum.
6. The committee marks up the bill and reports it out of committee.
7. The bill is debated and voted on in the originating chamber.
8. If approved, the bill is sent to the other chamber where it is introduced by the other cosponsor.
9. The bill is referred to committees for consideration.
10. Committee hearings are held to discuss the bill in a public forum.
11. The committee marks up the bill and reports it out of committee.
12. The bill is debated and voted on in the second chamber.
13. If no significant changes have been made to the bill in the second chamber, it is sent to the president for signature or veto.
14. If there are significant differences in the two versions of the bill, a committee is formed to reconcile the differences.
15. When identical bills have passed in both chambers, it is sent to the president.
16. If the president vetoes the bill, the legislature may attempt to override the veto by calling for a roll call vote in both chambers.

Source: Amidei, 2002; Bardes, Shelley & Schmid, 2006.

- Work with the media to draw attention to proposed laws and build public support.
- Testify to the merits of or the negative aspects related to proposed legislation.
- Offer alternatives to existing policies and legislation.
- Maintain awareness of federal, state, and local budgets and lobby for or against passage of various items (Adapted from Amidei, 2002).

Specific information about each of these activities will be discussed in Chapters 6, 7, and 8.

Lobbying

Another way to influence the legislative process is through **lobbying.** Lobbying is an open, established part of the process of influencing legislation and legislators. Major interest groups, such as the automobile or television industry often hire lobbyist who work, on a full-time basis, to influence executive and legislative decisions. However, any citizen or group of citizens can lobby. Lobbying is a protection written into the U.S. Constitution so that all citizens can make their views known to those elected to represent them.

The object of lobbying is to influence legislators and others with the power to regulate agencies that influence the quality of life for children and families. Effective ways to lobby include:

- Developing fact sheets, reports, and analyses that provide information to those in the position to influence public policy.
- Bringing together large numbers of constituents whenever there are public hearings or town hall meetings.
- Organizing letter writing (e-mail) campaigns that flood policy makers with the ideas and desires of their constituents.
- Working with the media to provide coverage of important issues and events.

Specific skills related to lobbying tactics mentioned above will be discussed in Chapter 7.

Understanding and Tracking Legislation

In order to effectively influence the legislative process, an advocate must read and understand the proposed bill and track it through the legislative process. We have previously pointed out that it is important to track a bill because it can be changed significantly and there are multiple opportunities for the bill to die. You can ask your legislator's office for copies of bills and committee reports, but it is often more timely to use the U.S. Congress's Web site, called Thomas (after Thomas Jefferson), http:// thomas.loc. gov. This site, sponsored by the Library of Congress, provides information about the status of bills as they pass through the legislative process. When you look up a bill using the assigned number, you will see the bill itself, names of its sponsors, the committee it has been assigned to, and the dates of hearings as they are scheduled.

Tracking a bill through the authorization or funding process is an important advocacy strategy because when you are aware of the timing of a hearing or vote you can develop letter writing campaigns or stage demonstrations that bring attention to the crucial action that is about to take place. Many advocacy groups develop advocacy agendas that outline impending legislative action as it relates to their particular issues and concerns. They then track the legislation and notify their members with **action alerts.** These action alerts tell the members exactly when to act, whom to contact, and what message to give. Individuals can join listservs and receive regular updates regarding legislation. Through its Web site, www.naeyc.org, The National Association for the Education of Young Children (NAEYC) operates *Children's Champions.* At this site, advocates can join an e-mail list and receive regular updates and action alerts on important issues, e-mail congress directly, find information about legislation and policies at the federal level that affect young children, and link to other organizations representing state policy makers. Figure 5.2 provides an example of an advocacy agenda and Figure 5.3 lists national organizations, other than NAEYC, that offer such services.

Figure 5.2 NAEYC's Advocacy Agenda for the 110th Congress

The NAEYC Call to Action for the 110th Congress addressed four areas:

A High-Quality Work Force
Provide grants to states, through reauthorization of the Higher Education Act, to design, coordinate, and implement a comprehensive workforce career system.

Provide grants to states, through the reauthorization of the Higher Education Act, to expand assistance for higher education to compensation increases as well as giving compensation rewards for staff with higher education who remain in the program.

Provide, through the reauthorization of the Elementary and Secondary Education Act (No Child Left Behind), joint professional development for teachers of young children in schools, child care, state-funded pre-kindergartens, Early Head Start, and Head Start.

Provide, through reauthorization of the Elementary and Secondary Education Act (No Child Left Behind) professional development for school principals, district superintendents, other district administrators, and central office staff.

A Continuum of Positive Development and Learning
Create, through reauthorization of Head Start, birth-to-five programs.

Create, through the reauthorization of the Elementary and Secondary Education Act (No Child Left Behind) early childhood educational teams in

(continued)

agencies and elementary schools to engage in joint professional development and ensure high-quality programs.

To align standards, curricula, and assessment for scaffolding learning achievement through the reauthorization of the Elementary and Secondary Education Act (No Child Left Behind).

To suspend, through Head Start reauthorization, the Head Start National Reporting System.

A Systems Collaboration to Support Young Children and Families

To establish in each state, through Head start reauthorization, a State Early Learning Council.

An Expansion of Access to High-Quality Programs

Provide, through budget resolution and appropriate legislation, a significant infusion of additional federal dollars for the Child Care and Development Block Grant.

Provide, through budget resolution and appropriate legislation, a significant infusion of additional federal dollars to expand access for families and children to Head Start and Early Head Start Programs.

Make, through tax legislation, the Dependent Care Tax Credit refundable and provide a larger credit for families using child care programs that attain national accreditation or a high level on the state quality-rating system.

Source: Adapted from *Making a Difference: Excellence in Early Childhood Education—Recommendations to the 110th U.S. Congress*, NAEYC, 2007.

Figure 5.3 Action Alerts

The following national organizations monitor funding and policy proposals related to child care, nutrition, education, and health care for young children. Their Web sites provide legislative updates and action alerts.

Alliance for Children and Families
www.alliance1.org
The Alliance tracks federal legislation on child abuse prevention and interventions, social services for low-income families, mental health, and other family-friendly supports.

American Academy of Pediatrics
www.aap.org/advocacy.html
The American Academy of Pediatrics monitors changes in Medicaid, SCHIP, and other health care programs and policies that benefit children.

American Association of School Administrators

www.congressweb.com/cweb4/index.cfm?orgcode+AASA

www.aasa.org. Click left hand menu "Policy & Legislation."

The American Association of School Administrators tracks legislation affecting students with disabilities and school-based health services.

Children's Defense Fund

www.childrensdefense.org

The Children's Defense Fund analyzes the impact of proposed federal legislation on ensuring that every child has a healthy start, head start, fair start, safe start, and a moral start.

Connect for Kids

www.connectforkids.org

The Connect for Kids Weekly e-newsletter provides weekly updates on new data, research, evaluations and public policy debates on a wide range of children's issues—from child care, to health, education, financial security, and safety.

Families USA

www.familiesusa.org

Families USA keeps track of funding and policy decisions that make a difference for children's health care.

Fight Crime: Invest in Kids

www.fightcrime.org

Because quality child care and preventing child abuse are key to reducing youth crime, this advocacy organization tracks federal legislation to improve access to quality care.

National Association of Children's Hospitals

www.childrenshospitals.net. Click left hand menu on Child Advocacy.

The National Association of Children's Hospitals monitors public decisions that affect health services for children.

National Head Start Association

www.nhsa.org. Click left-hand menu "advocacy."

The National Head Start Association monitors proposed changes and funding for Head Start and other early learning programs.

Influencing the Executive Branch

As discussed previously, agencies related to the executive branch of government are charged with turning the vague language of law into regulations which become the rules that actually govern the day-to-day operation of the programs created by the law. Advocacy groups can ensure that programs operate as they should on an on-going basis when advocates undertake the following tasks:

- Serve as volunteers in programs funded by the government.
- Serve on agency advisory boards and monitor program operations.
- Participate in the decision-making process of an agency.
- Comment publicly on the effect of regulations on citizens.
- Call for comments from elected officials related to proposed or existing regulations.
- Educate the public regarding proposed regulations.
- Challenge regulations when they prove inconsistent with the law (Amidei, 2002).

Influencing the Judiciary Branch

It is also possible to influence the Judiciary branch of government. Whereas advocates cannot try to influence judges through lobbying, they can use other tools such as lawsuits, complaints, and Friend-of-the-Court briefs that are useful.

Lawsuits often lead to better conditions for children and families. For example, a lawsuit forced the Social Security Administration to make children with autism, mental impairments, and other severe disabilities eligible for Supplemental Security Income (SSI). The effort took over seven years but has resulted in more than 500,000 children from families with modest incomes who now receive financial support (Amidei, 2002). Sometimes, just the threat of a lawsuit by a prominent advocacy group can initiate changes in the way systems operate.

Citizen complaints often lead to judiciary action that prompts agencies to review their processes or procedures. Advocates can help others file an *administrative appeal* when they feel that someone's rights have been denied.

Another way to influence the judiciary system is to initiate or sign a *Friends-of-the-Court brief*. This document describes the views of people that have direct knowledge of the impact a court decision is likely to have. Courts at all levels are interested in maintaining a broad spectrum of public opinion from citizens as it relates to matters facing the courts.

Joe Sohm/Chromosohm/Stock Connection

Voting is an important advocacy strategy.

Becoming an Informed Voter

Voting is an effective strategy all citizens can use to advocate for causes that are important to them. **Informed voters** will be able to make decisions about candidates and ballot initiatives that positively affect young children and their families. Before going to the polls make every effort to understand the impact of the ballot initiatives you will vote on. Learn about the candidates and know where they stand on important issues that affect children and families. Attend debates about important issues and pose questions. Support candidates and issues that you believe in by volunteering to work on their campaigns. On Election Day, help others get to the polls to vote.

SUMMARY

Advocates attempt to implement, challenge, or reform policies that affect the well-being of children and families. In order to do this, individuals act as experts, advocates, or community members. Effective public policy advocates understand the legislative process and work with advocacy networks to influence the formulation of policy at every step of the process. By becoming an active and informed voter, all citizens can act as advocate for causes they believe in.

RELEVANT CONCEPTS

public policy

constituents

case advocacy

administrative advocacy

legislative advocacy

class advocacy

expert

funding streams

authorizing bills

reauthorization bills

appropriation bills

tracking legislation

champion

lobbying

action alert

informed voters

FOR FURTHER READING

Constitutional Law by Erin Chemerinsly, 2006. Published by Aspen Law and Business.

Stir It Up: Lessons in Community Organization and Advocacy by Rinku Sim and Kim Klein (Eds.), 2003. Published by Wiley & Sons.

LINKS TO ADVOCACY RESOURCES

League of Women Voters

www.lwv.org

Provides objective information on current issues. Also, local chapters provide information of voting and service records of individuals running for office.

National Conference of State Legislatures

www.ncsl.org

Links to each states web legislative Web site.

Thomas

http://thomas.loc.gov

www.house.gov (or www.senate.gov)

U.S. Congress's Web site is called Thomas, named for Thomas Jefferson. This site provides information from the Library of Congress on bills including bill sponsor, bill status, congressional committees, congressional hearings, individual members— including their committee assignments—and schedules for the House and Senate.

QUESTIONS FOR REFLECTION AND DISCUSSION

1. Who represents you? Find Web sites that give you information about your municipal, state, and federal representatives. Are the views of your representatives, as they relate to policies affecting children and families, similar to your own?

2. What federal or state policies affect your life as a student or how you do your job as a teacher? How can you influence a change in these policies?

3. Distinguish, through example, the difference between a citizen's role in influencing public policy development and an advocate's role.

4. Lobbying isn't always as formal or official as it was described in this chapter. We all lobby for things we want or need. When was the last time you effectively lobbied for something? What skills did you use to get what you needed? Have you ever been ineffective in lobbying? Contrast effective and ineffective lobbying.

ADVOCACY IN ACTION: APPLICATION ACTIVITIES

1. Log onto the National Council for State Legislatures Web site (www.ncsl.org) and navigate the site to find all the information you can about your state. Write a brief report about an important piece of legislation now pending in your state. How will this legislation impact the lives of young children and their families?

2. Log onto the Web site for the National Association for the Education of Young Children (www.naeyc.org) and click on "Action Center." Navigate through the site and write a brief report about the opportunities this site has to offer advocates.

3. Join the Children's Champion Network and subscribe to the e-mail list. Read daily alerts and follow through on suggested activities to support one cause of interest. Write a brief report reflecting on your experience and detailing your action.

4. Choose from among the Action Alert Web sites listed in Figure 5.3. Log onto the site and navigate through. Choose an issue, provide a brief background for that issue, and describe pending legislation related to the issue.

Part II Developing an Advocacy Agenda

CONNECTIONS

As you read newspapers and news journals and listen to local and national news, what are some of the themes related to the well-being of children that reoccur? How can you learn more about these issues?

Profile of an Advocate

Paul Rasheed is a child development specialist at a mental health clinic in the Midwest. As part of his professional responsibilities, he plans and implements family education classes throughout the community. Paul had read about the national trend related to an increase of obesity among children and adolescents and understood it to be an overwhelming problem in scope and complexity. Many factors were involved, including advertising policies of large corporations, the trend toward electronic recreational practices among youth, food programs in schools, the lack of recreational programs in communities, and the personal habits of children and families. The frame of the problem was enormous and it was difficult to see how one person could impact the issue effectively.

When Paul learned that two of his own children were classified as overweight by their pediatrician, he became curious about the scope of the problem in his own community. He polled the families enrolled in his education classes and was surprised to find that 23 of the 38 children or adolescents were, by medical standards, overweight or obese. He knew that in order to impact the issue in any way he had to become fully informed. He interviewed his own children and the children in his family education program. He was curious to find out the children's perceptions related to why they had become overweight and what repercussions they were experiencing. He also surveyed parents to learn their perspectives related to their children's weight and the effect this had on the family's lifestyle.

Paul reviewed the current literature related to childhood obesity. He also interviewed a pediatrician and the recreation director for the local YMCA. He studied the Web sites of nonprofit organizations that were campaigning for policies that would stop the trend toward obesity among children. He considered the policies and practices of the families and schools of the children he was working with and of the general community, looking for correlations. He found that his initial perception was correct; the issue was indeed complex and multifaceted. There would be no easy solutions, but as he researched this issue, he met many interested individuals and learned about existing advocacy efforts. He was not alone in his concern and would not be alone in his advocacy efforts.

The more informed he became about how the issue of obesity played out in his community, the better he was able to reframe the enormousness of this problem and develop long and short term goals that reflected his capacity to act as an advocate. For example, one facet of the problem in his community was the public's lack of awareness of the resources available that would help them develop a healthier lifestyle. Therefore, he formed an advocacy group and together they implemented a campaign called Family Walk Fest. This event was scheduled for the first Saturday of every month at a local park. Those who attended engaged in activities that were fun for the whole family, and they could choose refreshments from vendors that offered a variety of healthy foods. They also received literature on healthy lifestyle choices from information booths sponsored by local agencies.

The campaign continued to evolve and had a positive impact on policy decisions made in local schools and on personal decisions made by many families. Although Paul was not able to completely resolve the issue of obesity in his community, by becoming an informed advocate, aware of his own capacity, he was able to reframe an overwhelming issue into an advocacy agenda that he and others in his community could tackle effectively.

Advocates like Paul Rasheed are people who recognize issues and policies that negatively impact children and families. Even when these issues prove to be overwhelmingly complex, advocates do not accept the status quo. They do not merely comply with policies they believe are harmful. Instead, they study the issue or policy carefully and develop the ability to view the issue from the perspective of all stakeholders. Effective advocates recognize their own capacity and are able to collaborate with others to reframe multifaceted issues, into malleable goals. In this chapter, we will discuss processes related to recognizing and becoming informed about the holistic nature of issues affecting young children and families, understanding one's own capacity, and reframing problems in ways that help others work collaboratively to implement equitable solutions.

RECOGNIZING PROBLEMS

One skill effective advocates have is the ability to identify conditions, issues, and policies that negatively impact children and families and also understand their interrelatedness. A condition is a major cause for concern. It is broad in scope and creates multiple issues that impact many individuals. Poverty is a condition that exists throughout the global society. It is the **root cause** of issues that are often dealt with through policies developed at the municipal, state, and federal levels. For example, the development and funding of programs such as universal prekindergarten or health care are responses to the condition of poverty.

Any one person would become overwhelmed by the idea of eliminating a condition as broad as poverty. The issues created by conditions like poverty, obesity, or the under education of a workforce are so broad in scope that they have to be dealt with through a variety of strategies and across multiple government and private agencies and advocacy groups. To be effective, advocacy efforts aimed at any condition will need to cross many contexts. That is, advocacy must occur with individuals, in both the public and private sectors, within programs, and even in the global arena.

Effective advocates understand the relationship between conditions and the issues they create. For example, poverty is often the root cause of poor nutrition which, in turn, impacts a child's performance in early care and education programs. As you begin to see this connectiveness, you can narrow the frame of the problem, and focus on what you can do with your skills and resources.

Early childhood professionals are often in a position to recognize policies that will negatively impact children and families. These policies may be created to combat a large-scale condition but, when implemented, prove ineffective or even harmful. For example, an elementary school administrator initiates a *no recess policy* thinking that this would give more time to academic studies and therefore increase the academic success of students. However, a policy of *no recess* can have many negative consequences for children. For example, the policy prevents children from having the opportunities to learn in an informal and outdoor environment. It has the potential to create stressful learning environments because children do not have the opportunity to release pent-up energy. And, it hampers teachers' attempts to create rich, integrated curricula that support teaching the whole child.

Because the early childhood professional understands the relationship between play and learning, she is compelled not only to identify the negative effects of this policy on children's opportunities for learning and development, but also to work toward establishing more appropriate policies that satisfy both the policymakers' needs and the needs of the children.

The first step in the development of effective advocacy is to thoroughly research the background of an issue or, in this case, an existing policy. You understand its intention and the perspectives of those who created or currently enforce it.

FINDING BACKGROUND INFORMATION

Before you are ready to determine what you can do about an issue or policy, you must become informed, that is you must develop a holistic understanding of the problem. "There are few worse advocates than people with good intentions and bad information. Good advocacy plans are based on solid facts, not anecdotes, guesses, or whatever happened to make it into the media" (Amidei, 2002, p. 37). The research you do when you first develop an advocacy agenda will result in a more effective focus and therefore more efficient strategies. If there were ever a situation in which the old proverb *a stitch in time saves nine* applies, it is at this step of the development of an advocacy plan. Being an informed advocate will save you much time and energy. It will lead you to others working on similar issues and allow you to capitalize on their energy and experience. Figure 6.1 is an initial list of questions that an advocate must investigate in the process of becoming an informed advocate.

Defining the Issue

In the beginning, define the issue with a simple description or narrative about what you know and why you believe it is a problem for children and families. Mr. Rasheed defined the obesity issue by a count of children in his immediate circle who were overweight. He added his impressions of how this condition was affecting them. As he learned more about the problem through his research, he included details, enriching his description.

Figure 6.1 Essential Questions

1. How is the issue defined? What is known about its origin? Its scope? Is it a local, regional, state, national, or global problem?

2. What policies or barriers exist that could block potential solutions to the problem?

3. What relevant theories exist that explain the problem or support potential solutions to the problem?

4. What is the current research base related to the problem or a potential solution to the problem?

5. Who are the stakeholders? That is, who has a vested interest in the solution to the problem?

6. What other advocacy groups are working on solutions to this problem? Who do you know that is interested in resolving this issue?

In the example concerning the *no recess policy,* an initial definition of the problem could consist of the circumstances surrounding the implementation of the policy and the concern for negative consequence. As the research on this issue continues, details are added. *For example,* what is known about the policy's origin? What is its scope? Do other schools have similar policies?

Discovering Existing Policies or Barriers

As part of the research related to issues you are concerned about, you will need to determine whether there are any existing policies that govern actions or create barriers that detract from positive solutions. If there are, you will need to determine their origin and the perspective of those who developed them. We often hear people refer to *they* when talking about policies or rules that are unpopular. And, we often make assumptions of who *they* are without knowing specifically where the policy came from or why it was implemented.

To find the origin of a policy, you can engage in an activity called **backward mapping.** When you backward map, you trace the policy's history to determine when and why it was developed and what the ultimate **source of authority** is. For example, if you were an early childhood teacher in the school with the *no recess policy,* before you can begin to plan how to revise or eliminate the policy, you would need to find out its origin. Was it really the principal who created the policy, or did it come from a higher source of authority such as the school board? And is it really a policy at all? That is, does it have a source of authority? Can it be enforced? Many times, teachers or other professionals operate from rules that they only think exist. These rules may have existed at one time, or the perception that there are rules may be based on simple traditions; for example, *It is just always done this way here*. When you trace the history of a policy and eventually come to its original source, you may find that there really is no rule at all, or that there is a policy but it has been misinterpreted.

You can begin tracing the history of a policy by simply asking questions and listening carefully to the responses people give you. Your purpose at this point is not to question authority but to understand the perspective of all **stakeholders,** that is, all individuals or groups that are affected by the policy.

Go first to who you think the source of authority is and ask them what they know about the policy. You could find out that who you think *they* are, thinks *they* are someone else. For example, you might think that the principal is the source of authority of the *no recess policy*. However, when you talk informally with her, you find that she thinks this policy was a directive of the school board. When you talk informally to school board members, or read minutes of related school board meetings, you find that the board never initiated a *no recess policy*. What they initiated was a call for more efficient use of instructional time. After talking to teachers in other schools, you find that several principals in the district developed a *no recess policy* to answer that call. Your principal may have adopted the policy of other principals because she thought it was a mandate or, indeed, she thought it would increase teaching time, or maybe out of a general concern for safety. The process of backward mapping takes time and patience, but you will uncover many interesting perspectives, and also some misconceptions, as you proceed.

Barriers are obstacles that prevent something positive from happening. They differ from rules or policies in that no one person or entity is responsible. For example, family involvement in a child's education is an important factor in quality programs and often leads to successful outcomes for children. For families with low-incomes (there is the initial condition of poverty again), transportation is often cited as a barrier for participation in school activities. In order to develop effective advocacy strategies that foster family involvement, the advocate must recognize transportation as a barrier and consider this when designing involvement activities.

Determining the Stakeholders

There will be several groups of stakeholders affected by the problem you have identified. These include **constituents,** the people you can bring into your advocacy campaign (note this term had a different definition than in Chapter 5) because they care about the issue and will be directly affected by the results of advocacy; **allies,** the people who will support you but may not be active in your campaign; and **opponents,** people who will work to prevent your success (Gay-Straight Alliance Network, 2008).

It is important to note that not all advocacy campaigns will encounter opponents because advocacy is often focused on improving conditions for children and families, and no one really opposes that. However, there will be **targets** for advocacy efforts. An advocacy target is the person or group with the power to grant you what you need to accomplish your advocacy goal. In the case of the *no recess policy,* the primary target is the principal. Secondary targets can also be identified. These are people who may have more power over the primary target than you do, but who you have some influence over (Gay-Straight Alliance Network, 2008). In this example, a secondary target may be parent leaders of the school Parent-Teacher Association. They may have more influence over the principal than you do, but you are in a position to influence them.

Determining the Perspective of Stakeholders

As you trace the history of a rule or policy you will begin to identify the stakeholders, individuals who have a vested interest in the policy. Certainly in this case of the *no recess policy* the school board is a stakeholder, as is the principal. But there are other stakeholders also. Teachers, children, and families associated with the school are all affected by the rule and therefore they are also stakeholders. It is important to understand the **perspective** of the stakeholders as it relates to the rule or policy. Effective advocates find out how all stakeholders feel about the different aspects of the problem. This is done most effectively through direct communication techniques such as interviewing, surveying, or conducting focus groups, not by making assumptions, and not by arguing your case. Returning to the example of the *no recess policy* you may have assumed that the principals were trying to eliminate play because they did not understand or value the educational benefits of play. However, you don't really know until you interview them. And, of course, you are going to find multiple perspectives among any group of individuals. Figure 6.2 suggests questions that will reveal the perspectives of stakeholders.

It is not always possible to seek out the perspective of all stakeholders. For example, parents and children are stakeholders in many of the issues advocates care about but are not always aware of the potential problems or may not be able to articulate their concerns. In the field of early childhood education, teachers are given the responsibility to represent the interests of infants, children, and families. It is important that teachers, acting as advocates, be accountable to those they represent and not just express their own ideas. Nobody likes to be spoken for without being consulted. This is an especially sensitive issue if the stakeholders are not mentally competent, frightened, overwhelmed, or in any other way unable to speak for themselves. Infants and young children fall into this category. Once you understand the perspectives of multiple stakeholders, you can begin to develop solutions that speak to or satisfy the concerns of all involved.

Another way to develop firsthand knowledge about problems and gain the perspective of stakeholders is to participate as a volunteer with organizations that are working to resolve issues that affect infants, young children, and their families. Chapter 10 provides details of how volunteerism leads to informed advocacy.

Figure 6.2 Understanding the Perspective of Others

1. What is the stakeholders' general understanding of the policy or issue in question?
2. What personal values does the stakeholder connect with the policy or issue in question?
3. How are those personal values being supported or threatened by the issue or policy in question?
4. What information does the stakeholder need to be able to reconsider his feelings about the issue or policy in question?

RESEARCHING TOPICS

After you have gathered the needed background information, you should begin to research topics related to the issue. As stated in questions 3 and 4 of Figure 6.1, you will want to determine what relevant theories and current research exist that support plausible solutions to the issues you defined. A good place to begin is by reviewing professional journals and position statements.

When conducting research, particularly when using the Internet to locate material, it is important to be discriminating when choosing articles because postings on the Web are often opinion, not fact. However, by being a critical reader and knowing the source of the information you are reading, you can filter out sites that are pure opinion and focus on those that support their ideas with credible research data done by reputable organizations and whose articles are **peer reviewed.** Peer-reviewed articles are those that are read and critiqued by experts in the associated field, then revised by the author before publication. Peer review is a standard practice of professional journals and adds credibility to the ideas and findings presented. You can determine if a journal is peer reviewed by reading the front matter where the ownership, purpose, and editorial practices are described.

When researching a problem, it is important to balance your reading between articles that reflect **primary sources** of information—that is, articles that are written by those actually doing research in the field or

Researching issues thoroughly is a vital step that results in effective and informed advocacy strategies.

are creating theories related to the problem and those that represent **secondary sources** of information. Secondary sources are articles that interpret and synthesize the work and ideas of others. They are also valuable resources because they lead you to understand how concepts and ideas are interrelated and are applicable in broader contexts.

You may want to extend your research efforts by studying Web sites sponsored by professional organizations and nonprofit child advocacy organizations. These sites include background information on many problems

Figure 6.3 Advocacy Organizations

Annie E. Casey Foundation
www.aecf.org

Children's Defense Fund
www.childrensdefense.org

Child Welfare League of America
www.cwla.org

Easter Seals
www.easterseals.com

Families First
www.familiesfirst.org

Federation for Children with Special Needs
http://fcsn.org

Fight Crime: Invest in Kids
www.fightcrime.org

Parent Advocacy Coalition for Educational Rights (PACER)
    Champions for Children with Disabilities
www.pacer.org

Stand for Children
www.stand.org

The National Center for Children in Poverty
www.nccp.org

United Way of America
www.unitedway.org

Zero to Three
www.zerotothree.org

facing families, statistics that outline the scope of the problem, references to both primary and secondary sources of information, and links to other related sites. Figure 6.3 provides a starting point for using the Web to supplement research related to many problems affecting young children and their families.

If your advocacy efforts are related to educational practice, a good place to begin a search is on the Web site of professional organizations such as Association of Childhood Education International (ACEI), International Reading Association (IRA), and the National Association for the Education of Young Children (NAEYC). These and other professional organizations regularly publish position papers related to many issues facing educators today. These position statements provide a synthesis of current research and theory related to a topic and also a bibliography that is useful for furthering your investigation. In addition to position statements, most organization's Web sites offer peer-reviewed articles

Figure 6.4 Web Sites of Professional Organizations

Division of Early Childhood, Council of Exceptional Children
www.dec-sped.org

International Reading Association
www.ira.org

National Association for the Education of Young Children
www.naeyc.org

Association for Childhood Education International
www.acei.org

National Association of Bilingual Education
www.nabe.org

National Association of Elementary School Principles
www.naesp.org

National Association of State Boards of Education
www.nasbe.org

National Black Child Development Institute
www.nbcdi.org

National PTA
www.npta.org

Figure 6.5 Position Statements

International Reading Association
www.ira.org
> Literacy Development in the Preschool Years
> Using Multiple Methods of Beginning Reading Instruction
> Developmentally Appropriate Practices for Young Children

National Association for the Education of Young Children
www.naeyc.org
> Antidiscrimination Statements
> Code of Ethical Conduct and Statement of Commitment
> Conceptual Framework for Professional Development
> Developmentally Appropriate Practice
> Developing and Implementing Policies to Promote Accreditation
> Early Childhood Curriculum, Assessment, and Program Evaluation
> Screening and Assessment of Young English-Language Learners
> Early Childhood Mathematics: Promoting Good Beginnings
> Guiding Principles for Development and Analysis of Early Childhood
>> Public Policy
> Inclusion
> Learning to Read and Write
> Licensing and Public Regulation
> Media Violence in Children's Lives
> Prevention of Child Abuse
> Quality, Compensation, and Affordability
> Responding to Linguistic and Cultural Diversity
> School Readiness
> Standards for Professional Preparation Programs
> Still Unacceptable Trends in Kindergarten Entry and Placement
> Technology and Young Children
> Violence in the Lives of Children

Association of Childhood Education International
www.acei.org
> Resolution on Childhood Obesity
> Play's Role in Brain Development
> Separation of Church and State
> What Parents Need to Know about Standardized Testing
> Statement on Children and War/Peace Education
> Statement on the Use of Child Soldiers
> The Child's Right to Creative Thought and Expression
> Play: Essential for All Children
> On Standardized Testing

related to specific issues facing infants, young children, and their families. Figure 6.4 provides the Web address of several professional organizations and Figure 6.5 provides a list of position statements available from NAEYC, IRA, and ACEI.

CONSIDERING YOUR OWN CAPACITY

After thoroughly researching the background of the problem, you will come to understand why it exists; who is affected by its existence; what rules, policies, or barriers are present that prevent resolution; and what the perspectives of stakeholders are. You are almost ready to develop an advocacy agenda. However, before considering the possible solutions and actions you could take, consider your own **capacity,** that is, your talents, skills, and resources (Amidei, 2002). It is important to develop a true sense of your capacity so that you can set an advocacy agenda for yourself that is both challenging and achievable. You do not want to overestimate your capacity, but you certainly don't want to underestimate it either. Figure 6.6 outlines questions you can ask yourself to help determine your capacity for action.

Each time you take on an advocacy effort you will increase your capacity because you will have developed new skills and new contacts. Therefore, it is important to reevaluate your capacity each time you take on a new challenge.

Figure 6.6 Determining Your Capacity for Advocacy Work

How much passion do I have for this issue?

How well do I understand the general problem and the perspectives of the stakeholders involved?

How much time can I devote to this effort?

Who are my constituents and allies?

What advocacy groups are already conducting campaigns related to this issue?

What contacts do I already have that will support my efforts?

What monetary resources are available?

What talents and skills do I have that will support the resolution of this problem?

FORMULATING ADVOCACY AGENDAS

Advocacy agendas are well-informed plans related to resolving issues that negatively impact infants, toddlers, young children, and their families. Advocacy agendas are proactive, contain specific objectives, both short- and long-term goals, and are flexible. They are regularly reviewed and revised. Advocacy agendas present positive solutions to stakeholders and therefore invite them into the process of resolving the issue. Since everyone has a stake, everyone emerges a winner.

Let us return to the example of the *no recess policy* stated earlier in this chapter. The advocate in this example determined from her research that (a) play is a viable learning strategy, (b) the policy was created to increase the learning potential of all students, (c) there is a precedent for recess being used as a learning experience; other schools have ongoing programs and are willing to share them, and (d) she has the enthusiasm, energy, and knowledge about play to develop a recess program that will highlight informal learning. Therefore, she developed an advocacy agenda focused on collaborating with grade-level teams to develop and implement a recess program that links outdoor play activities to specific learning goals. In doing this she presented an alternative to the no recess policy that is specific and theoretically achievable. It takes into account the position of all stakeholders and invites them to join a conversation about maximizing the learning potential of students and the resources of the school. When this program is implemented and proves to be successful, all stakeholders will share the credit. Therefore, this advocacy agenda becomes one more effort aimed at improving overall school success.

Advocacy efforts do not end with reframing problems into advocacy agendas. Much work will still need to be done to get others to buy into suggested solutions. But presenting proactive alternatives is a strong first step. In the next chapters, we will discuss specific strategies advocates use to bring other stakeholders on board and collaboratively work toward positive solutions.

SUMMARY

There are many overarching problems in the world that create negative factors that affect the lives of infants, young children, and their families. Finding a single solution to any of these problems is not only overwhelming but also virtually impossible. Effective advocates go beyond mere compliance when they come up against policies that negatively impact children and families. They work toward solutions by gaining a thorough understanding of the problem and the perspective of all stakeholders. With this information, and after considering their own capacity, they reframe the problem into advocacy agendas which are proactive, flexible, and theoretically achievable.

RELEVANT CONCEPTS

root cause

backward mapping

source of authority

stakeholders

barriers

constituents

allies

opponents

targets

perspective

peer reviewed

primary sources

secondary sources

capacity

advocacy agenda

FOR FURTHER READING

Educators on the Frontline: Advocacy Strategies for Your Classroom, Your School, and Your Profession by Jill Lewis, Kathleen Stumpf Jongsma, and Allen Berger, 2005. Published by the International Reading Association.

LINKS TO ADVOCACY RESOURCES

Coalition of Infant/Toddler Educators

www.njcite.org

This coalition promotes quality infant/toddler care and education.

The National Prekindergarten Center

www.fpg.unc.edu/~NPC

Provides research policy analysis and community and technical assistance for decision makers who implement prekindergarten programs.

Mentor/The National Mentoring Partnership

www.mentoring.org

This organization promotes, advocates, and is a resource for mentors and mentoring initiatives.

The Children's Partnership

www.childrenspartnership.org

National research policy analysis and advocacy organization focused on children and technology, children's health issues, and building a broader constituency to support children's issues.

QUESTIONS FOR REFLECTION AND DISCUSSION

1. Review articles in your local newspaper that report about the instances of crime in your local community. Also listen to local news reports and pay attention to how crime is reported. Discuss the possible root causes of the crime in your community and how this crime may be affecting children and families. Brainstorm ways to reframe the issue of crime and create potential advocacy agendas that would help resolve some of the issues that are negatively affecting children and families.

2. If you were to pursue an advocacy agenda that was related to the condition of juvenile crime, what background information would you need to obtain and what theoretical knowledge would you need? Where would you begin your search for this information?

3. Working in groups, choose one of the issues listed in Figure 4.2 of Chapter 4. Discuss what might be the root cause of the issue. Who would be the major stakeholders associated with this issue? List the background information you would need to understand the issue thoroughly. How would you obtain this information? What theoretical knowledge would you need? How would you obtain this? What advocacy groups might be working to resolve similar issues?

ADVOCACY IN ACTION: APPLICATION ACTIVITIES

1. After reviewing local newspapers or viewing local news programs, identify a policy or rule that you believe impacts (positively or negatively) the lives of

infants, young children, and families in your community. Trace the origins and intentions of this policy through backward mapping.

2. Think about an issue related to the development of a strong after school program in your community. Identify the stakeholders. Distinguish among constituents, allies, and opponents. Who might be primary and secondary targets in a campaign?

3. Locate a professional journal in your library and search the front matter to determine editorial policies. Is this journal peer-reviewed? What topics are covered in the journal?

4. Choose two Web sites from Figure 6.3 and compare the contents of these sites as they relate to providing background information for studying problems that affect infants, young children, and their families.

Chapter 7: Choosing Strategies

CONNECTIONS

When you need to raise awareness about an issue, what strategies can you use? How would you go about changing someone's mind?

Profile of an Advocate

When Aubyn Burnside was 10, she learned that when foster children moved from home to home they often had to carry their personal belongings in black garbage bags. She was so moved by this disturbing idea that she began collecting suitcases to donate to the Catawba County Department of Social Services. This was not just a random act of kindness on her part but an organized effort to do something about a condition that affected children her own age. Aubyn founded a project called *Suitcases for Kids*. She spread the word by speaking to local 4-H clubs, Boy and Girl Scout troops, and Sunday school classes. She published information explaining her program in church bulletins and local newspapers and she posted notices at libraries, schools, and on community bulletin boards.

After only 5 months, she was able to deliver 175 reconditioned suitcases to the Department of Social Services for distribution to foster children. Aubyn then partnered with the *Families for Kids Program,* which was funded by the W. K. Kellogg Foundation. She developed a 12-page "starter kit" that gave background information on the project, steps to replicate the program, press releases, reminder notices, and thank you letters. Her project first expanded statewide and then nationwide. Today, *Suitcases for Kids* (www.suitcasesforkids.org) is an international nonprofit organization that aims to educate people to donate their used luggage so it can be recycled and given to individuals with a need. Aubyn's story illustrates that not only can one person make a difference, but when that person joins with others, real solutions can be found that have a positive impact on people's lives. (Source: http://suitcasesforkids.org/history.htm, downloaded 3/27/07)

To be effective, advocacy must be both intentional and strategic (Robinson & Stark, 2002). Aubyn Burnside's actions were intentional, that is, she had studied the situation and knew exactly what she wanted to accomplish. Barbara Dixon (Chapter 1) and Gretchen Renaldo (Chapter 2) were also very intentional in their advocacy efforts. However, these three advocates all used very different strategies to accomplish their goals. Identifying issues, becoming informed about their holistic nature, and reframing them into a proactive advocacy agenda are important first steps in effective advocacy. The next step is to develop and implement strategies that can be used to accomplish the task. The purpose of this chapter is to describe different strategies and discuss the contexts in which they are most effective.

STRATEGIES AND TACTICS

Strategies and **tactics** are the specific actions you take to accomplish your advocacy agenda. All issues are complex; therefore, a combination of strategies will be needed to create organized and flexible agendas. Strategies can be grouped into three broad categories (Amidei, 2002). **Educational strategies** are used when your objective is to help the general public, or a specific group, gain an awareness or better understanding of an issue. Educational strategies will probably be needed in all advocacy agendas. For example, as we advocate for our profession, we will need to educate the public about the important role of early childhood professionals. When you want to change an advocate policy, you will need to educate policymakers about the specific factors that are negatively impacting children and families.

Persuasive strategies are used when your objective is to promote or dissuade the development of specific rules or policies. For example, to defeat the *no recess policy* described in Chapter 6, the advocate had to not only inform stakeholders of the value of recess (but also persuade them to use recess as a learning opportunity to resend the policy). In advocating for the profession, we also have to both inform the public of the importance of early education and persuade policy makers to increase funding for quality programs.

Mobilization strategies are used to (1) get your message out and/or (2) keep your message alive in the minds of both policy makers and the general public. Mobilization strategies often connect you with other groups that are doing similar work. In this chapter, we will discuss educational and persuasive strategies that are effective when working with policy makers from both the public and private sectors. Mobilization strategies will be discussed in Chapter 8.

EDUCATIONAL STRATEGIES

If a better understanding of a problem or issue is necessary to implement your advocacy agenda, you will need to use educational strategies to inform both the public and policy makers. Fact sheets or briefs, letters to the editor, Web sites, position papers, and reports, are examples of educational strategies. Their purpose is to inform policy makers and the general public of the need for certain actions, policies, or programs. Two general principles apply when creating educational material: (1) target a specific audience and (2) maintain high credibility by presenting well researched facts (Lewis, Jongsma, & Berger, 2005). Figure 7.1 lists educational strategies useful in many advocacy initiatives.

Fact Sheets/Briefs

Fact sheets and **briefs** inform the reader about an issue through a highly organized one-page (or two pages printed back to back) document. They begin with the most poignant facts about the issue and list them in a bulleted format. When creating fact sheets or briefs, you will want to make them readable by using a 12-point font, bold type, text boxes, and graphics to highlight important points. Also, make clear what you want readers to do. For example, you may want the reader to contact their legislator or

Figure 7.1 Educational Strategies

Fact Sheets/Briefs
Web Sites
Reports
Position Papers
Information Kits
Letters to the Editor/Editorials for the Opinion Page
Surveys and Public Opinion Research
Multimedia Presentations

---

school board member to speak for or against a certain initiative. Provide all information the reader will need to speak clearly about the issue. Finally, give references or links that would direct the reader to resources that would lead to a greater understanding of the issue or suggestions for further action.

You will need to make several different versions of a fact sheet so that you can target different audiences. Remember, different stakeholders perceive issues from different perspectives and therefore may need to be approached in unique ways. Good examples of fact sheets can be found on many nonprofit advocacy Web sites. Check specifically Campaign for a Commercial Free Childhood, www.commercialfreechildhood.org. Click on Facts.

Web Sites

In this technological age, it is easy to develop a Web site that represents your ideas as they relate to a matter concerning infants, young children, and their families. Web sites are often developed by individuals who support certain causes. Professional groups often devote a section of their Web site to advocacy. It is easy to target different audiences on a Web site by placing links that lead visitors to facts and articles that are of particular interest to them. For example, if you are developing a Web site to support the development of employee child care facilities in both public and private companies, you could offer a specific menu for parents and another one for company executives. The parent's link would lead to reports outlining the benefits of employee child care, position statements from professional societies, and fact sheets that spell out action steps for working with company executives to develop child care centers. The company executive's link would lead to reports that provide specific examples of successful facilities, fact sheets that outline the benefits, and specific information about developing facilities. Figure 7.2 provides good examples of Web sites designed to support advocacy issues.

Reports

Reports are written documents that provide a general overview of a particular issue, topic, or problem. They often include a history of the problem, a statistical analysis related to its prevalence, and a review of related

Figure 7.2 Web Sites That Support Advocacy Issues

Fight Crime: Invest in Kids

http://fightcrime.org

This Web site is sponsored by police and sheriffs in many different states and offers valuable information to parents about keeping children safe after school. It also tracks federal legislation to improve access to quality care.

California Kindergarten Association

http://www.ckanet.org

This site is committed to facilitating quality education for all kindergarten children and includes information of conferences, grants, publications, and current legislation.

Love Our Children, USA

www.loveourchildrenusa.org

This site is dedicated to fighting child abuse through outreach, advocacy, and education. It offers publications and resources for parents, kids, and teens.

Children's Alliance

www.childrensalliance.org

This site is sponsored by an advocacy organization dedicated to improving the health, safety, and economic well being of the children in the state of Washington.

Southern Institute on Children and Families

www.thesoutherninstitute.org

www.kidsouth.org

This site is dedicated to improving the lives of low-income children and families.

---

research. Reports are generally written by experts in a field, are objective, and offer a range of possible solutions with explanations of the pros and cons of each. You can write your own report or search the Web for reports written by highly credible agencies.

Position Papers

Position papers are specific documents that outline an organization's philosophy on a particular issue. These papers provide essential information in an easily accessible format and can be used to develop fact sheets and other material needed to educate policy makers. Many professional organizations regularly publish position papers or reports that are useful in educating the public about different issues in education. Figure 6.5 lists different position papers that can be found on the Web sites of professional organizations.

Information Kits

Information kits are a combination of fact sheets, reports, and position statements that are left with policy makers or the general public after a visit or event (Benson, 2000). Each kit should include material that highlights your main points, charts, and graphs that support your position and a list of specific actions you want the reader to take. They can be assembled using different combinations of materials to target different audiences You can also include buttons or pencils with a special slogan that represents your issue. Always include a contact sheet with an information kit so that individuals can get in touch with the advocacy group that sponsored the event.

Letters to the Editor and Editorials

Letters to the editor are personal responses to a previous article in the paper or a current situation or event in the community. They are short and to-the-point, usually about 150–200 words. "Letters to the editor are a good way for professional educators to be active links between the public and the educational community" (International Reading Association, 2007, p. 33). Letters can be written to praise actions of community members or policy makers, to correct misconceptions or inaccuracies, or to bring public attention to an issue. An example of a letter to the editor written to draw public attention to the importance of early education is provided in Figure 7.3.

An **Editorial for the Opinion Page** (op-ed) is longer, from 500 to 1,000 words, and is formatted as a provocative, timely essay that expresses your opinion on an important issue in a way that informs the public and calls them to action. It is true that many papers reserve the op-ed pieces for well-known writers, editors of other papers, or officials, but a well-written essay on a relevant topic will always be considered.

Because of the brevity of these formats, you must plan your message carefully. Figure 7.4 provides guidelines for writing and submitting letters to the editor.

Before publishing, editors will contact you to confirm your identity and the fact that you wrote the piece. After the letter is printed, it is a good strategy to send copies to targets of your advocacy agenda. In fact, when you see other letters or editorials that support your advocacy, copy, and save them. They will prove useful when you develop persuasive strategies.

Figure 7.3 A Letter to the Editor

Education Reform Begins in the Nursery
Re: "Quality Counts for Children," Our Opinions, Aug. 15

The Gazette-Times Editorial stated the need for reform in the city's elementary schools to enhance the future of all children. However, children are born learners and the years from birth to 5 are critical to the development of language, thinking, motor, and social skills. Therefore, waiting until children begin school to help them develop necessary skills and dispositions is waiting too long. Comprehensive program providing family education to families of infants and very young children need to be developed and implemented across our community.

Research shows that infants and children who are read to consistently develop strong literacy skills and develop them early. It is true; what happens at home and in child care centers during the first three years of life builds the foundation for later learning.

As we work to develop high quality schools, we must also support families in becoming their childrens' first and most important teacher.

Raul Tamedia
Kindergarten Teacher
Robert E. Davis Elementary School
Coos Bay, Oregon

Surveys and Public Opinion Research

Statistics and other information gained from surveying a specific group of citizens will provide impressive information for policy makers. There are many online data sources that will help you develop these fact sheets. Some are listed in Figure 7.5.

Often, however, when dealing with a specific school, community, or neighborhood, important statistics are not readily available. For example, if your advocacy plan includes working with the city's department of recreation to develop a neighborhood park in an underserved area, you may not be able to find all the specific information you need about a particular neighborhood from public sources. You could, however, develop a survey and canvass the affected neighborhoods to gather information about the number of families with young children who would utilize such a facility. In the survey you could ask families how they see the park improving

Figure 7.4 Guidelines for Writing Letters to the Editor

1. Review the submission guidelines for the specific paper you are submitting to. They can usually be found on the "letters to the editor" page.
2. If you are responding to a particular article, identify that article clearly at the beginning of your letter.
3. Plan your message carefully and, in doing so, choose one or two focal points.
4. Identify yourself. For example, "I am a kindergarten teacher at Adams Elementary. I am also the mother of two young children."
5. Avoid jargon. Don't say. "DAP is the best way to provide a quality education for young children." Instead use language that everyone understands, "By matching the content and expectations of activities to each child's unique ability, we are fostering further development in important areas such as thinking, reading, and using mathematics."
6. Write from a personal perspective. Use real-life examples and stories to engage the reader and get your point across.
7. Check your facts. Be sure you are accurate so that you maintain credibility for your profession.
8. Propose a solution. Say what needs to be done to address the problem you are describing. Do not become angry or inflammatory. Speak reasonably, always promoting a proactive message.
9. Include your name, address, a phone number where you can be reached, and any appropriate organization affiliation.

Sources: Amidei, 2002; Benson, 2000; IRA, 2007; NAEYC, 2004a.

their lives and their interactions with their young children. You could publish the results by developing a fact sheet and report that includes the data and supports your plan to create a public playground in this neighborhood.

Multimedia Presentations

Available technology, such as PowerPoint, make multimedia presentations easy to prepare and present. Presentations can include photographs and film as well as interviews with individuals who are or would be affected by pending policies and legislation. It is important to target the presentation to specific audiences and leave this audience with an information kit that provides reports, fact sheets, and reference information.

Figure 7.5 Data Sources

U.S. Census Bureau
http://www.census.gov

Kids Count
www.aecf.org/kidscount/

Child Trends Data Bank
http://childtrendsdatabank.org

Children's Defense Fund
www.childrensdefense.org

Federal Interagency Forum on Child and Family Statistics
www.childstats.gov

National Center for Education Statistics
www.nces.ed.gov/

National Child Care Information Center
http://www.nccic.org

PERSUASIVE STRATEGIES

"Facts alone rarely persuade politicians. Organized voters using facts in politically savvy ways often do" (Amidei, 2002, p. 60). Persuasive tactics are designed to educate and influence public and private policy makers through direct contact. Often, policy makers are called upon to make decisions with limited or even biased information. Advocates and advocacy groups can provide information that is current, specific, and is based on actual experience. Through face-to-face interactions, that is, through lobbying, citizens can influence legislators, school boards, or other policy makers to create new policies, repeal or modify existing policies, and/or support funding for existing policies.

> Whereas advocacy just means speaking up, lobbying (which is one form of advocacy) concerns communication with an elected official (or staff), which conveys a position on a piece of legislation. It is how everyone from paid professionals to average citizens can make their views known to decision makers about a pending or proposed change in public policy. Lobbying is a protection written into our Constitution. (Amidei, 2002, p. 24)

The object of lobbying is to use whatever power or influence you have to influence decision makers (Benson, 2000). Effective lobbying begins with thorough research. It is not only important to know the essential facts about your issue or policy, but to also know the opposition's arguments, understand all possible compromises, and be ready to negotiate. It is important that you pick the targets of your lobbying efforts carefully. Some policy makers will be on your side from the beginning, others will need a little persuasion, and still others will never come around to your point of view. We can identify five different stands of policy makers who may take on any issue. They are described here:

1. **Champions:** Policy makers who are already dedicated to your cause. They will lend you their support and may be able to influence other policy makers on your behalf.
2. **Allies:** These are policy makers who are generally on your side but can be influenced to do more; to be more outspoken about their support for your issue.
3. **Fence Sitters:** These individuals are uncommitted on your issue. They can potentially vote for or against you. These are the key targets for your lobbying. They can be persuaded.
4. **Mellow Opponents:** These individuals will work against your issue when it comes up but are not inclined to become active against your issue.
5. **Hard-Core Opponents:** These are the policy makers who are leading or aligned with your major opposition (Schultz, 2003).

Effective lobbying can be accomplished through visits, letters and e-mails, phone calls, and by providing testimony at public meetings. Because policy makers deal with hundreds of issues each year, your role as an educator and early childhood advocate is very important. Your expertise in the area of child development and education can make a significant contribution to the development of sound public policy.

> The object is not to be liked, but to be respected and heard. At the heart of the process is the perception of power—who had it, how it is wielded, who wins, who loses. Money is not necessary to convey power; commitment, persistence, voters, the ability to attract the media—all are forms of power available to advocates. (Amidei, 2002, p. 25)

Figure 7.6 lists persuasive tactics useful in shaping both public and private policies.

Figure 7.6 Lobbying Strategies

Visits
Letters and E-mails
Phone Calls
Testimony
Hosting Policy Makers

Visits

"Establishing face-to-face contact with each elected official is one of the most effective methods to influence public policy" (Benson, 2000, p. 8). An important first step in establishing a working relationship with policy makers is to know who represents you and who is responsible for making and upholding policies related to your school or community, or to the state and federal programs that you are concerned about. Certainly, your principal or program director represents you within your school administration. But who represents you on the school board and city council? Who are your state representatives, both in the house and in the senate? Who represents you in the federal government?

A second step in forming viable relationships with policy makers is attending Town Hall meetings or other public functions where your representatives are present. Listen to their ideas and opinions. Look up their voting record on the Internet. Take every opportunity to introduce yourself to policy makers and their staff as both a constituent, someone they represent in a policy-making capacity, and as an expert in the field of early education. Do not be shy. Constituents always have a right to meet with their representatives, and policy makers need to know the views of their constituents.

When it comes time to lobby for a specific issue you will want to visit key policy makers and express your concerns and your expectations for their action. You will need to find out where your representatives stand on issues concerning education and young children and families so that you can target your visits appropriately. Are they champions of your cause? If they are, you will want to thank them for their support and urge them to influence their fellow policy makers on behalf of the issue. Or, are they allies or fence sitters? If this is the case you will need to be more persuasive

Effective advocates know policy makers and meet with them whenever possible.

in your message and implicit about how and why you want them to act. It is important to carefully choose whom you visit and have a specific goal in mind for each visit. Focus your time and attention on the fence sitters and mellow opponents. These are the people that are most susceptible to your message. Enlist allies and champions to work with you. Figure 7.7 lists points to consider in planning and carrying through with a visit to a policy maker.

Letters and E-mails

Writing policy makers is another effective lobbying technique that allows you to make your views known. Letters and e-mails are most effective when they arrive at the time a particular issue is being discussed. Professional groups, like NAEYC, will send out legislative alerts to their members when key bills are under discussion or are up for voting. This is the time to voice your ideas. Personal letters are more effective than form letters because you are able to include personal testimony or anecdotes that

Figure 7.7 Planning a Visit to a Policy Maker

Prior to the visit
- Choose who you will visit and establish a specific purpose for the visit.
- Research the issue and develop a correlation between what you are asking and the interests of the policy maker's constituency (i.e., what does his/her voters have to gain if he/she supports your issue?) (IRA, 2001, page 9)
- Research the policy maker's background and voting record as it relates to the issue.
- Develop fact sheets that clearly show the effect of the issue in the policy makers region.
- Anticipate any questions you might encounter and be prepared to answer them. That is, know the position of the opposition and be ready to refute these points.
- Prepare a 3–5 minute statement that outlines your position and states exactly what you want the policy maker to do.
- Put together an information kit to leave with the policy maker.
- Select a delegation to go with you. Limit the group to 3–6 members and select a diverse group. It is important to include a parent who has a compelling story that relates specifically to the issue. Make sure all members of the delegation are part of the policy maker's constituency.
- Make an appointment. Identify the issue you want to discuss and your position. If you intend to take a member of the press with you, establish this fact when you make the appointment.
- If the policy maker cannot meet with you, ask to meet with the staff person who works with the issue that you are representing. Do not be disappointed. Policy makers rely on staff for information. Meeting with staff can prove as powerful as meeting with the policy maker.
- Rehearse the meeting with your delegation so everyone knows what to expect.

During the visit
- Be on time but be prepared to wait.
- Address the policy maker with the appropriate title, thereby keeping the meeting at a professional level. Remember it is your meeting because you asked for it, so you take the lead in the agenda and maintain a schedule of 15–20 minutes.
- Introduce yourself and your delegation noting both your relationship as constituents and your expertise or point of interest as teachers, parents, and citizens.
- Thank the policy maker for taking time to see you and for their interest in the issue.
- Give your prepared statement concerning the issue.
- Listen carefully to the policy maker's concerns or opinions for opportunities to provide information or clear up misconceptions.

- If you are asked a question you cannot answer, state that you do not know but will find out and communicate it through a phone or e-mail message.
- Conclude the meeting by reiterating what it is you want the policy maker to do regarding the issue.
- Offer your expertise as a resource to their staff.
- Invite the policy maker or key staff person to visit your program or school if that is pertinent to the issue you discussed.
- Again, thank him for his time and leave an information kit that provides more information and contact numbers for all members of the delegation.

After the visit
- Within three to five days of the meeting, send the policy maker a letter which summarizes the visit, provides answers to any unanswered questions, and thanks her for her time and efforts regarding this issue.

Source: Adapted from Benson, 2000; International Reading Association, 2007; NAEYC, 2004a.

portray how a particular policy affects the people in your community (International Reading Association, 2007). Figure 7.8 provides suggestions for writing effective letters and e-mails.

Phone Calls

Phone calls can be as meaningful as visits, letters, or e-mails when they are timed to reinforce your views regarding a specific issue or pending policy decision. It is important to be prepared before you make a call. You might want to write a short script that includes

1. The appropriate salutation for the person you are calling,
2. Your name and your relationship as a constituent,
3. The specific bill number or name or the policy you are calling about,
4. Your expertise regarding the issue,
5. Why the bill or policy matters to you and to the policy makers constituents. This could include a specific example or anecdote that puts a "face" on the issue,
6. What you are asking the policy maker to do,
7. What the policy maker's position on the issue is,
8. An offer to testify or send additional information (Benson, 2000; International Reading Association, 2007; NAEYC, 2004a).

Figure 7.8 Writing Letters and E-mails to Policy Makers

- Time your letter to coincide with discussion and voting on specific policies that relate to the issue.
- Use the appropriate title in your salutations.
- Begin with a brief statement that outlines your position concerning the issue. Include the specific name or bill number of the policy in question.
- Establish your credibility as it relates to the issue by describing your expertise, professional position, or experience.
- Provide a brief and constructive discussion of the issue offering solutions to problems. Describe how these solutions would positively affect the community.
- Support your position with anecdotes from your classroom or community that helps the policymaker put a "face" on the issue.
- Explain exactly what you want the policy maker to do in regard to the issue or bill.
- Keep the letter brief, between 1 and 2 single-spaced typed pages. You can include pertinent editorials or stories from the newspaper or fact sheets.
- Ask for a written response to your letter.
- Conclude the letter by thanking the policy maker for his time and effort on the behalf of the issue.
- Include your name, name of the organization you represent, address, and phone number.

Source: Adapted from Benson, 2000. International Reading Association, 2007; NAEYC, 2004a.

Conclude with thanking the policy maker for his or her time. If it is not possible to talk to a specific policy maker, ask to talk to the staff person who is working on behalf of a particular bill or issue. Never be disappointed when you talk to a staff person instead of the policy maker. Remember these are key people and policy makers value their ideas and opinions. Figure 7.9 contains a sample of an effective phone message and Figure 7.10 provides contact information for senators and representatives.

Testimony

Educators can and should offer to testify at hearings designed to elicit public response to pending legislation or other public policies. **Testimony** may be given before legislative committees, school boards, community councils, or even the boards that govern service agencies such as YMCAs and community food banks. Notices of public hearings are published in

Figure 7.9 Effective Phone Calls and E-mails

> Good Morning. My name is Barbara Stumph and I am a constituent of Senator McKinzie. I would like to speak to the senator or to the staff person who is following the current Head Start reauthorization legislation. I believe that it is important to provide a continuum of developmentally appropriate curriculum and assessments as well as meaningful family engagement for children, birth through early elementary school, and their families. I also believe that Head Start is a viable program for accomplishing that goal and I am asking that Senator McKinzie support the reauthorization of the Head Start bill when it comes up for a vote.
>
> Please send a written response to Barbara Stumph, 2037 Green Avenue, Medford, OR, 97594. My phone number is 555-277-9513. Thank you for attending to this matter.

newspapers prior to the meeting. It is important to notify the committee conducting the hearing that you or a spokesperson from your advocacy group wishes to testify.

In choosing a spokesperson, select someone who has the appropriate expertise, gained through education and/or experience, and is not only articulate but also able to handle difficult questions with ease and grace (Benson, 2000). Offering testimony at hearings requires careful preparation because each witness is generally limited to 5 or 10 minutes.

Figure 7.10 Contacting Your Congressional Representative

> To contact your U.S. Senator or Representative, address your correspondence as follows:
>
> The Honorable _____
> U.S. House of Representatives
> Washington, D.C. 20515
> Dear Representative_____
>
> The Honorable_____
> U.S. Senate
> Washington, D.C. 20510
> Dear Senator_____
>
> Call the Capitol switchboard at (202) 224-3121 and ask to be connected to your senator's or representative's office.

Figure 7.11 Guidelines for Giving Testimony

1. Greet and address your audience using the appropriate nomenclature.
2. Introduce yourself by name and position as it relates to the matter at hand.
3. State clearly, from the beginning, what your position is.
4. Design your remarks around only 3 or 4 major points and get right to them. Do not take a long time to set the stage. Get right to the point.
5. Do not use professional jargon. Consider your audience when selecting your words and define concepts in ways all will understand easily.
6. Use memorable anecdotes and compelling stories to illustrate your points without becoming overly emotional or dramatic.
7. Practice many times before you are called to testify. Do not read your testimony verbatim because you will lose eye contact with your audience and the passion that you feel for your issue will be lost. Do bring an outline that you can refer to.
8. Repeat your major points in your conclusion and provide a clear statement of what you want the committee to do.
9. Be prepared to answer questions. If asked something you do not know, state that you do not have this information but you will provide it. Then follow up and send all members of the committee the requested information.
10. Thank the committee for their time and consideration.
11. Bring written copies of your testimony to distribute to both the committee and the audience. You may also want to bring along and distribute fact sheets or information kits.

Source: Adapted from Benson, 2000.

Figure 7.11 provides guidelines for developing and delivering testimony in public hearings.

Hosting Policy Makers

Members of Congress are often asked to *ride along* with police or firefighters. Such events provide policy makers with firsthand knowledge and experience that often clarifies misconceptions or inaccuracies. These visits reinforce the need for specific policies that support first responders when carrying out their crucial mission. Early childhood educators also have a critical mission related to developing and maintaining a healthy community. We can emulate the positive outcomes of ride alongs by inviting key policy makers to visit early childhood programs. These visits can (1) raise the awareness of policy makers to critical issues related to early education and (2) if the media is invited, also, raise the awareness of the general public.

> Too few elected officials understand the connections between high-quality early education and school readiness. In addition, many have misconceptions about the realities of the child care programs. Many think that because parents pay high tuition that centers are well resourced. Others think that teachers are well paid. Still others lack a clear concept for how greater public investment would specifically matter. (NAEYC, 2004a, p. 19)

Program visits that are strategically planned to emphasize important issues related to early education will provide policy makers with crucial information necessary to create and support sound policy. Policy makers are more likely to visit programs within their own jurisdiction, especially if they know parents and/or media will be attending (NAEYC, 2004a). It is also helpful if someone in the hosting organization, parent, teacher, or administrator, has a personal connection with the policy maker or a member of her staff. That is why it is important to take every opportunity to meet policy makers when they are appearing at public events.

Hosting public officials at your center or school is an effective advocacy strategy. These visits will help policy makers understand the needs of children and families.

133

Plan the event to reinforce a key message you want to relay (NAEYC 2004a). For example, if you want to influence state legislators to increase funding for prekindergarten education you should invite policy makers to visit a site that is striving to be a high-quality center but struggles to meet the highest expectations regarding resources, compensation, or affordability for parents. Be sure that the site represents diversity among the clientele. "It is critical to convey a message that transcends the specific site so the official walks away with a greater understanding about local child care needs not just a specific opinion about one child care center they visited" (NAEYC, 2004a, p. 40).

Develop an agenda and schedule for the visit and provide it to the visitor beforehand. Stick to the schedule, but always have a backup plan because policy makers often run late to appointments. Plan a tour and a brief presentation, but also give parents, teachers, and children an opportunity to interact informally with the visitor. Before the visit, help parents and staff strengthen their ability to communicate their goals for their children to policy makers.

As the visit concludes, provide written material that reinforces your key message. Also provide biographies and phone numbers of those that participated. As you thank the visitor for coming and say goodbye, reiterate exactly what you want the policy maker to do.

SUMMARY

Developing an effective advocacy plan means being both intentional and strategic. It involves choosing strategies that educate both the general public and policy makers about your issue. Educational strategies include fact sheets, Web sites, reports, position papers, information kits, letters to the editor or editorials, surveys, and multimedia presentations.

To implement your advocacy plan, you may need to go beyond educating and convince key policy makers to support your cause. Effective persuasive strategies include visits, letters and e-mails, phone calls, testimony, and hosting policy makers at your program, school, or center. All issues are complex. Effective advocacy efforts therefore require the use of many different educational and persuasive strategies.

RELEVANT CONCEPTS

strategies

tactics

educational strategies

persuasive strategies

mobilization strategies

fact sheets

briefs

reports

position papers

information kits

letters to the editor

editorial for the opinion page

champions

allies

fence sitters

mellow opponents

hard-core opponents

testimony

FOR FURTHER READING

Public Speaking for Success by Dale Carnegie and Arthur R. Pell, 2006. Published by Penguin Group.

Artful Persuasion: How to Command Attention, Change Minds and Influence People by Harry A.A. Mills, 2000. Published by AMACOM.

Psychology of Persuasion: How to Persuade Others to Your Way of Thinking by Kevin Hogan, 2003. Published by Pelican Publishing Group.

LINKS TO ADVOCACY RESOURCES

The following links lead to educational journals helpful in locating theory and research-based information related to educational issues.

American Education Research Association—Communication of Research

http://aera-cr.asu.edu/ejournals

The Web site provides links to online educational journals that provide access without membership fees.

Early Childhood Research and Practice

http://ecrp.uiuc.edu

This is a bilingual Internet journal focused on the development, care, and education of young children. It does not require membership.

International Journal of Teacher Leadership

http://www.csupomona.edu/ijtl/

This is a peer-reviewed online journal that deals with issues of leadership in education, including advocacy. It does not require membership.

QUESTIONS FOR REFLECTION AND DISCUSSION

1. You believe that your second-grade students need more independent center time than is currently offered in your school. You know you have three distinct groups of individuals you need to first educate and then persuade regarding the need for independent center time; the other second-grade teachers, the parents, and the administrator. Describe how you would develop educational materials to target each of these diverse groups. What strategies would you use to persuade each group to allow more time for center activities?

2. Policy makers will have different stands related to different issues. Describe ways you can determine where they stand on specific issues. Using the five categories of policy makers' stands described in this chapter, discuss who would be the best targets for a lobbying campaign. Why? Who would you not want to target? Why?

3. In the opening profile, Aubyn Burnside's advocacy actions benefited many individuals. These actions were not designed to affect public policies related to the foster care system. However, when advocacy actions are developed to influence public policy, maximum benefit can be realized. What kinds of policies could be developed to support foster children as they transition from one home to another? What advocacy strategies could be used to support the creation of such policies?

4. Discuss the ethics of involving children in advocacy activities. For example, would holding an event showcasing children in a child care center or inviting policy makers to visit educational programs—that is, using children as a means to an end, even if the end is intended to benefit them—be unethical? What are the ethical issues associated with involving children in advocacy activities? How can these issues be resolved?

ADVOCACY IN ACTION: APPLICATION ACTIVITIES

1. Define an advocacy issue that is important to you. Identify the policy makers who have influence on this issue. Find the policy maker's stance on the issue and design a campaign to influence this policy maker to support your issue, or if she already does, to influence her colleagues to support your issue.

2. Define an advocacy issue that is important to you, or continue to discuss the issue that you defined in Question 1. Develop and conduct a survey that would reveal the ideas and opinions of the stakeholders involved in this issue.

3. Find position papers and reports that relate to issues that are important to you. From these create two information kits, each targeted at a different audience.

4. Write and submit a letter to the editor in support of an issue that is important to you.

Chapter 8: Getting Connected—Staying the Course

CONNECTIONS

Thinking of issues that are important to you, who else might be interested in collaborating with you to resolve problems that affect children and families? How can you connect with these individuals or groups? How would you begin developing an advocacy strategy? How would you stay organized and flexible?

Profile of an Advocate

Pearlie Harris is the owner of Royal Castle Child Development Center in New Orleans, Louisiana. She is also the mother of six children, including a son with autism. Over the years, she learned how to work with school personnel to receive and maintain a high-quality education for her son. But it was after Hurricane Katrina flooded her child care center with 6 feet of water and devastated the child care network of New Orleans that she learned the importance of networking with individuals and collaborating with agencies to resolve issues facing her community. At first, Ms. Harris dismissed the possibility of rebuilding the center, but when her center's cook, also a general contractor, offered to help rebuild she began to think that it might be possible. She applied for a loan from the Small Business Administration, but her application was rejected because the business had been underinsured. She heard that the Federal Emergency Management Agency (FEMA) was giving money for critical services—including schools and libraries—so she began to search for someone to help her access these funds. Agenda for Children, a local child care advocacy group, however, also failed to access these funds because of bureaucratic red tape. Funds from the state Department of Social Services were restricted to the purchase of moveable supplies because of a requirement of the federal block-grant authority. In August 2006, 13 local organizations, including Agenda for Children and the United Way for the Greater New Orleans Area, formed a coalition—The Greater New Orleans Rebuild Child Care Collaborative. They were then able to raise several hundred thousand dollars and award grants, payable directly to contractors hired to rebuild the city's child care community.

However, Pearlie did not wait for the collaborative to be formed. She received construction assistance through the United Way's Success By 6 program and a grant from the Institute of Mental Hygiene. Volunteers assembled playground equipment donated by KaBOOM!™. Finally, she was ready to reopen her center and offer child care services for children 6 weeks to 7 years of age (information from Harris, 2007; Reckdahl, 2007).

The adage, "There is strength in numbers," is never as true as when it comes to advocacy. Collaborating with others to (1) share information and ideas, (2) get the message across, and (3) keep the message alive in the public consciousness is an important part of any effective advocacy plan (Amidei, 2002). Mobilization strategies help you get and maintain high visibility for your issue. They include joining together with others to form advocacy groups or coalitions, hosting events, and working with the media. These strategies rely on having a strong network of personal and professional acquaintances who can provide timely information and advice on issues relating to your advocacy and put you in contact with people who have the power to get things done. In this chapter, we will explore these mobilization tactics and then bring all the parts of an advocacy agenda together and discuss how to sustain momentum.

NETWORKING

Most advocacy issues are best tackled in league with others who have a vested interest in the outcome. A professional **network** is an important tool for advocacy because it enables you to connect with people who have ideas, information, or power, which will help you develop and implement your advocacy agenda. Networks consist of your colleagues and friends and their colleagues and friends. Your child's teacher is in your network, as is his pediatrician. Pearlie Harris had met many people associated with working with young children. Her network included other child care providers, college professors, graduate students, agency directors, officials from the state department, and many others. When it came time to develop and implement an advocacy agenda, she had the potential support of all these people and of all the people they knew. She was able to draw from this rich resource for information and ideas (P. Harris, personal communication, February 5, 2007).

Networks are developed informally and work informally. For example, Stamos Alexander is a first-grade teacher at a public elementary school. One evening, at a National Association for the Education of Young Children (NAEYC) affiliate meeting, he met and chatted with Dorothy Webber. Dorothy taught in an inclusive kindergarten in a nearby school district. Stamos noted that she was confident and enthusiastic about her work. Several months later, Stamos wanted to know more about inclusion. He remembered Dorothy, looked her name up in the affiliate directory, called her, and set up a meeting to discuss how to incorporate more inclusive strategies into his teaching. Dorothy brought material and names of other teachers who were working to develop inclusive classrooms. She gave him information about the Council of Exceptional Children (CEC). Stamos went to a meeting of the local affiliate of CEC and learned of the availability of grants for the implementation of inclusive practices. He went back to his school and worked with colleagues to develop a proposal that was funded. The state department learned of the work being done at Stamos's school and asked him to testify before a committee that was reading a policy proposal related to inclusive education. While preparing to testify, Stamos met with a legislator's aide and others in the position of developing or supporting policies that support infants, young children, and families. This example of networking has no end because networking continues throughout one's professional life. It is important to note that even though Stamos met Dorothy at a professional meeting, he could just have easily met her on the golf course. The line between professional networks and personal networks is blurred.

FORMING ADVOCACY GROUPS

As was stated earlier, there is strength in numbers. Groups not only have more power and visibility but have the capacity to get more done. It is essential to develop an **advocacy group** early in the process of implementing an advocacy agenda. Allison Piedmont was a second-grade teacher in an urban elementary school. Because she understood how important conversation is to the development of language skills among young children, she felt that a valuable opportunity for developing meaningful conversation was being blocked by a policy that prevented children from talking during their lunch period. Through backward mapping (Chapter 6), she determined that the rule was implemented by the building principal in order to maintain order and calm in the lunchroom. After talking among teachers in her school, she found four others who also believed that time in the lunchroom could be developed into meaningful language-learning experiences. Together, they formed an advocacy group, researched lunchroom policies across a number of schools in her district and state, and developed a plan that would group older and younger children together in *lunch families*. While in the cafeteria, the older children would sit with the younger children and discuss predetermined topics. School volunteers, including parents and senior citizens, would circulate among the families to facilitate conversation.

The group presented the plan to grade-level committees. Through **collaborative discussion,** problems inherent in the plan were identified and then resolved. The original plan underwent many levels of revisions. As these revisions occurred, support for the plan grew. More and more teachers came on board and supported the idea of a meaningful and pleasant lunchtime experience. The final plan was presented to the Parent–Teacher Association (PTA) and to the local chapter of Volunteers of America. After a full year and multiple versions, the Lunch Families Plan was implemented at Allison's elementary school.

What had begun as one person's idea became a **synergistic melding** of the ideas of many, resulting in not only a workable plan but a vested and shared interest on the part of many stakeholders. This is an example of **grassroots advocacy**—ideas for change begin with the people who are most involved, not the policy makers.

It is generally easy to find other constituents and allies (Chapter 6) to support your initial ideas. Start by looking within the system most affected. Allison looked within her school community because that is where this issue originated, but she soon networked with individuals from other schools. Stamos found his initial support outside his school community in his professional network.

If an issue is community based—for example, if you determine that a stop sign is needed at a busy intersection in order to keep neighborhood children safe while playing or crossing the street—you might first solicit support from parents in the neighborhood, form an advocacy group, and work both with the neighborhood association and with the city's safety

Figure 8.1 Finding Support for Issues

Consider the following individuals and organizations when deciding whom you might partner with to get support for your advocacy issues:

- Colleagues
- Teachers
- Building administrators
- Teachers' unions
- Parents
- Community volunteer groups
- Neighborhood associations
- Health care professionals
- Law enforcement personnel
- Faith-based organizations
- Civic and fraternal organizations
- Businesses
- Affiliate groups of professional organizations (i.e., NAEYC or Association for Childhood Education International [ACEI])

Sources: Lewis et al., 2005; Robinson & Stark, 2002.

bureau to get the needed sign. Figure 8.1 lists individuals and organizations that might provide support for advocacy issues that develop within your program community.

Managing Advocacy Groups

Once a group is formed, someone must take a leadership role and begin to develop a sense of purpose among the participants (Shultz, 2003). There will be many responsibilities to share among group members. These include:

- recruiting others
- researching the problem and solution
- defining goals
- developing strategies
- choosing effective tactics
- creating informative and persuasive materials
- maintaining focus and motivation
- fundraising, and
- being a spokesperson

Once the advocacy group becomes acquainted, it should be easy to match individual's skills to responsibilities.

Effective Meetings

Meetings provide a way to maximize a group's function. It is important to make the most of meeting times by having a clear agenda that is distributed before the meeting and by having a facilitator who can work for consensus among the group, manage conflict, and keep members focused on the ultimate goal.

> Having a prepared and disseminated agenda will help you manage your actual meeting time effectively. It will enable you to focus on the group so that by the meeting's end, good discussion will have been made and the meeting participants will know the next steps and when those steps need to be accomplished. Objectives for each meeting should be reasonable and achievable. You cannot accomplish everything at one sitting, and most individuals cannot focus for an extended period of time. Frequent, shorter meetings may accomplish more than those that are several hours long. (Lewis et al., 2005, pp. 91–92)

Conclude each meeting by deciding on the purpose, date, and location of the next meeting. Figure 8.2 is an example of a well-organized meeting agenda. Note that the person responsible for presenting and the time allotted for each item are noted on the agenda. This ensures that everyone comes prepared for the meeting, thus optimizing the time and energy available for advocacy.

COALITIONS

Coalitions are groups of organizations that have a vested interest in a particular issue and therefore join forces to reach a common goal (Benson, 2000).

> A coalition is an organization of organizations. Coalitions are not just a list of individuals: they represent the combined influence and support of multiple organizations—each of which have dozens or hundreds of members. (Amidei, 2002, p. 44)

Coalitions can help advocacy campaigns develop a stronger public image by bringing together networks of people from diverse backgrounds and providing them with a forum for thinking about community problems from varying perspectives. Through the formation of coalitions, resources,

Figure 8.2 Advocacy Group Meeting Agenda

Date: May 18, 2007
Time: 4:30–6:00
Place: Dawn Wheet's Home, 236 Broad Street, Madison, 555-958-1349

1. Welcome and introductions of new members (Paul, 3 min)
2. Approval of minutes from previous meeting (Paul, 2 min)
3. Announcements (anyone, 5 min)
4. Celebration of recent accomplishments related to advocacy plan (Emmy, 5 min)
5. Update on plans for community event (Robyn, 25 min)
   a. Brainstorm ideas for site
   b. Choose four sites and delegate a member to check each site
6. Review information packet materials (Marty, 25 min)
7. New business (Paul, 20 min)
8. Determination of time, date, and task for next meeting (Paul, 5 min)

including funding sources and volunteers, can be funneled to one cause, avoiding a duplication of effort. Coalitions also offer a mentoring mechanism for newer advocates (Shultz, 2003).

Coalitions can be structured at many different levels of formality. The most informal would be networks or lists of organizations and their members that support similar causes. These networks can be called upon when planning events to showcase a particular issue. **Ad hoc coalitions** are formed when one specific organization takes the lead in pushing a particular policy through a legislative process. The lead organization communicates with member organizations through newsletters and action alerts (Chapter 5).

As coalitions become more formalized, they may create membership criteria, hold regular meetings, and create their own agendas (Shultz, 2003). Coalitions often create a legislative or regulatory task force whose main function is to

1. report the status of bills, timing of hearings and votes to all members;
2. research legislators' position statement and voting records to determine their positions;
3. identify legislators to sponsor needed bills that will benefit coalition's constituency;

4. establish ties with the offices of the governor and mayor and offer to serve on special task forces that study issues related to coalition's advocacy agenda;

5. identify community groups that are addressing similar public policy issues and are willing to collaborate (Benson, 2000).

Figure 8.3 presents examples of national and international coalitions that support issues related to infants, young children, and their families.

When looking for organizations to join together in coalitions, you would want to ask yourself (1) what groups are already engaged in similar advocacy activities and (2) what groups can bring credibility, clout, and expertise to this effort? (NAEYC, 2004a). There are several national advocacy groups that maintain offices in each state. These organizations can be great partners to

Figure 8.3 Coalitions That Support Infants, Young Children, and Their Families

National Children's Coalition
http://www.child.net/ncc.htm
The NCC was established to advocate for a substantial and urgent effort to stem the growing crises among our kids: the child abuse, the alarming suicide rate among teens, violence directed at or by children, AIDS, and domestic violence.

National Coalition Against Domestic Violence
http://www.ncadv.org
National Coalition Against Domestic Violence's (NCADV's) mission is to organize for collective power by advancing transformational thinking and leadership of communities and individuals to end the violence in our lives.

Community Anti-Drug Coalitions of America
http://cadca.org
The Community Anti-Drug Coalitions of America (CADCA) is a membership-driven organization put in place to give antidrug and drug-related coalitions technical assistance and support.

Coalition on Children Affected by AIDS
http://www.ccaba.org/
This is an international coalition that works to bring awareness to issues that affect children with HIV/AIDS.

Injury Free Coalition for Kids
http://www.injuryfree.org
The vision of the Injury Free Coalition for Kids is that children and families will live in safer communities.

Figure 8.4 Coalition Partners

Association for Childhood Education International
www.acei.org

Children's Defense Fund
www.childrensdefense.org

National Association for the Education of Young Children, State Affiliate Groups
www.naeyc.org

National Parent Teacher Association
www.pta.org

Stand for Children
www.standforchildren.org

Voices for America's Children
www.childadvocacy.org

Zero to Three
www.zerotothree.org

smaller advocacy groups because they often have both resources and expertise to share. Figure 8.4 offers a sample of organizations, found nationwide, that would make good coalition partners for advocacy groups that support issues that affect infants, young children, and their families. Working with coalitions can be very beneficial in getting the message across to the public and to policy makers and in keeping the issue in the public eye.

HOSTING EVENTS

Joining together with others is one mobilization strategy. Another is hosting events that showcase your cause. Planning and carrying out events such as rallies, marches, or annual luncheons is a great way to bring public awareness to an issue or call for action from a body of legislators or other policy makers.

Rallies and marches are often thought of as protests, but they can be very positive and uplifting events when they honor infants, young children and their families, teachers, child care workers, or volunteers; or when they bring attention to child care programs, schools, or libraries (Lewis et al., 2005). These celebrations can be powerful when speakers focus their message on the needs of infants, young children, and their families and when the media is invited. Events can be sponsored by individual advocacy groups, by coalitions, or by individual schools or programs.

By providing ideas and resources to local groups, many national or international organizations support events that focus on the needs of infants, young children, and their families. NAEYC sponsors the Week of the Young Child. The national organization sets the date, usually in April, and the theme for the annual event. But each affiliate or program plans its own activities. The Association for Childhood Education International sponsors a Celebration of the Classroom Teacher. Again, the national organization sets the date, but local organizations plan and carry out their own events. Figure 8.5 provides examples of events that promote public awareness of advocacy issues.

Planning a successful event will take many months and much collaboration between members of a group or coalition. It may be necessary to work with city officials and the police to obtain the correct permits and security. Well-planned events leave a lasting impression both on the public and on policy makers. Figure 8.6 provides a list of Web sites to consult for additional information on national and international events that may be

Figure 8.5 Advocacy Events

- Invite a local legislator to speak at a luncheon honoring child care workers.
- Hold a virtual lobby day and ask all members of a coalition to contact their legislator via e-mail to promote the passage of a bill critical for funding of early childhood programs.
- Invite school board members to a school celebration of literacy. While they are present, have children and parents speak about the need for certain programs or policies being considered by the school board. (See Chapter 6 for a more detailed information on hosting a policy maker at your school.)
- Hold a celebration or children festival in a local park during the Week of the Young Child. Have community organizations manage information booths, thus providing resources to parents.
- Host a Celebration of the Classroom Teacher banquet and honor local teachers. Invite legislators who consistently support education initiatives as guest speakers. Invite the media.
- On the last day of a professional conference related to early education, hold a rally and carry signs that promote the passage of impending legislation that funds public health insurance.

Figure 8.6 Event Planning Guides

The Week of the Young Child
www.naeyc.org

Celebration of the Classroom Teacher
www.acei.org

Worthy Wage Day
www.ccw.org/about_WWpacket.html

The Great American Bake Sale
www.strength.org

Center for Screen Time Awareness
www.screentime.org (for information about TV Turnoff Week)

---

celebrated by local advocacy groups or early childhood programs. In the Links to Advocacy Resources section, there are links to Web sites that provide event planning tips.

WORKING WITH THE MEDIA

A third mobilization strategy is working with the media. Local media outlets will be a great resource for your advocacy efforts. Develop a rapport with these outlets as you develop your advocacy agenda. They will be helpful in getting your message to the public and to policy makers. Scour your local area for all media outlets. Do not be limited to the obvious—the local profit-based newspaper, radio, and television stations. In most areas, you will find smaller community service–oriented papers that are distributed to local businesses and restaurants, any place where people gather. You may also find public-access radio and television stations. Many agencies, including schools, PTAs, booster clubs, public health organizations, neighborhood associations, and fraternal organizations, publish newsletters and often welcome news articles that highlight issues and resources related to infants, young children, and their families.

Get to know these sources, and create a **media contact list.** Learn the names of reporters who cover educational issues. Add them to your network. Build proactive relationships by taking a media tour and introducing yourself to these important contacts. Learn about their audiences, news cycles, and deadlines. Explain your interests and offer your services as a resource.

Early childhood professionals are often interviewed by the press about issues that affect infants, young children and their families.

Michael Littlejohn/PH College

Preparing Material

When preparing materials for media sources, to be presented either in writing or through an interview process, be clear about what you are trying to achieve with your message. Are you trying to develop public awareness about a situation that needs attention? Are you trying to move people to action? Or are you trying to put pressure on policy makers? Figure 8.7 provides general guidelines for preparing material for the media.

Types of Media Coverage

There are many ways to get information out through the media. They include press releases, public service announcements (PSAs), and television and radio broadcasts. A brief discussion of each follows.

Press Release

A **press release** is a story or an announcement you submit to various media. In a press release you may give information about an upcoming event or tell a compelling story about the effect or possible effects a proposed policy may have on a group of infants, young children, and their families. Press releases should be limited to a page and a half. After sending the release to the appropriate media sources, follow-up with telephone calls to your media contacts. When articles appear, cut them out and send them to the appropriate policy makers.

Figure 8.7 Preparing Materials for the Media

1. Know exactly what you want to say. Write down two or three clear statements before you talk to the press. Stay "on message."
2. Give clear, concise, and accurate data. Lead with the most important points.
3. Know the exact date, time, and location of events before you contact reporters.
4. Do not use acronyms or professional jargon. Use language the general public understands.
5. Use metaphors or anecdotes to illustrate your point. Make them personal, that is, give a "face" to the issue, but do get permission beforehand.
6. Know your oppositions' points and be ready to refute them with facts.
7. Go beyond discussion of the problems and present solutions.
8. Make your story newsworthy, that is, human, current, and compelling. Link it to something else that is already a big event in the news.
9. Be prepared for requests for additional information and follow through promptly.
10. For written submissions, double check spelling and grammar.
11. Include contact information so reporters can call with questions.

Source: Lewis et al., 2005; NAEYC, 2004a; Schultz, 2003.

Public Service Announcements

A **public service announcement (PSA)** is a 10- to 90-second message that is broadcast free by radio and television stations as a service to the community, thus fulfilling their obligation, as outlined by the Federal Communications Commission, to serve the public interest. Many PSAs are produced by professional production companies, but it is also possible for local groups to create a script and submit it to the station. An announcer then reads the copy on the air. The International Reading Association (IRA) suggests that when submitting PSAs, you should include the following:

Organization name, address, and telephone number

Name of publicity contact and telephone number

Start and stop dates for the PSAs to air

Length in seconds

Typed, double-spaced copy to allow for easy reading

Phonetic spellings of any name or word that is difficult to pronounce (IRA, 2007, p. 38).

The following is an example of a PSA created by the IRA to promote reading to infants:

> Even the youngest child can enjoy books. Infants delight in having poems and rhymes read to them as they are bounced on a parent's knee. This has been a message from the International Reading Association. (IRA, 2007, p. 40)

Broadcast Media

Broadcast media, such as talk radio and cable television, can offer timely opportunities to get your advocacy messages out. Listen to programs on the local talk-radio stations and find out what topics are generally presented. When you find a program that is child and family friendly, prepare your message, call, and keep trying. If you can offer to answer a previously asked question or provide additional information on an ongoing topic, your call may be taken (IRA, 2007). Public-access channels will broadcast information from citizens about events and community services via a community bulletin board. Contact your local station for guidelines on submissions.

IMPLEMENTING AN ADVOCACY AGENDA

In Chapter 6, we defined an advocacy agenda as the overall guide used to reach your advocacy goals. It is a clear assessment of where you are, where you want to go, and how you want to get there. Previously in this text, we discussed these essential components of an advocacy agenda or plan:

- A complete understanding of the issue (Chapter 6)
- Identification of stakeholders and their perspectives (Chapter 6)
- Identification of champions, constituents, allies, and opponents (Chapters 6 and 7)
- Primary and secondary targets for advocacy (Chapters 6 and 7)
- Long- and short-term goals (Chapter 6)
- Networks and coalitions you can work with (Chapter 8)
- Educational, persuasive, and mobilization tactics (Chapters 7 and 8).

Once these components are in place, it is time to organize all activities and develop the last component of the advocacy plan—the **timeline.**

The first step in developing a timeline is to brainstorm a list of everything that needs to be done to complete your agenda. After the list is generated, sequence items in a logical order and set realistic dates for completion. When setting due dates for tasks, you may need to consult the legislative or school calendar. Complete your timeline by delegating responsibility for each task on the list. Match the tasks to the individuals in your network who possess the greatest capacity to fulfill them successfully.

Maintain Vigilance and Flexibility

Advocacy work needs to be sustained over time. To do this, keep abreast of any changes related to your issue. Stay in touch with your network. Schedule regular meetings with your advocacy group and share information and experiences. Review and adjust your overall advocacy strategy and your timeline often. Be flexible; but do not give up! Policy change is incremental, and it will take time and consolidated efforts to make even a little bit of progress, so be prepared to stay the course.

One way to maintain a positive attitude and prevent burnout among your advocacy group is to recognize and celebrate every step toward your goals.

> So when should you celebrate? Anytime you have accomplished something that gets you closer to your advocacy goals! Be grateful for the small successes along the way as well as the big outcomes that may have long lasting and wide-ranging effects. (Lewis et al., 2005, p. 223)

Examples of "small successes" include the following:

- Your building administrator asks your opinion about a policy issue because she recognizes your expertise in an area.
- People who have heard you speak on an issue ask you for more information.
- You are cited in a newspaper article related to your issue.
- Your PSA gets repeated airtime.
- A slogan your group developed to promote your issue becomes known.
- Your opposition begins to recognize the merits of your campaign.
- A reporter asks you or someone in your group for an interview (Lewis et al., 2005).

As you maintain vigilance, be willing to compromise and negotiate your demands. Small steps are better than stalemates when it comes to promoting

Celebrate all victories no matter how small they may seem.

policies that affect infants, young children, and their families. And always celebrate positive government actions publicly with letters to the editor and thank-you notes (Amidei, 2002; Lewis et al., 2005; NAEYC, 2004a).

Figure 8.8 presents a worksheet that will be helpful in developing and revising advocacy plans. This plan represents an initial stage in Allison's development of the Lunch Families Plan. Plans will necessarily be revised many times during the course of an advocacy. A blank worksheet is available in the Appendix.

SUMMARY

Mobilization strategies are essential during the developmental and implementation phases of advocacy. These strategies include collaboration with others and forming advocacy groups and coalitions, hosting events, and working with the media.

The essential components of an effective advocacy agenda or plan include a complete understanding of the issue; the knowledge of stakeholders and their perspectives; and the identification of constituents, allies, and opponents, primary and secondary targets for advocacy, long- and short-term goals, networks and coalitions you can work with, educational, persuasive,

Figure 8.8 Advocacy Planning Worksheet

Strategic Plan for Advocacy

Date Initiated *September 2006* **Advocacy Group or Individual** *Allison*

Statement of the Problem *Children learn language through conversation, but at this time a significant portion of the time they spend in school is unavailable for conversation. That is their 30-min daily lunch period.*

Background Information *The no-talking lunchtime policy was implemented in 2002 by Principal Manning after many complaints from parents that children were not eating their lunch. Cafeteria monitors had also complained about general rowdiness in the cafeteria. The principal developed the policy so that children would have a safe and quiet period in which to focus on their eating. At present, this rule is strictly enforced, but it does result in many confrontations, power struggles, and reprimands. Even though the cafeteria is quiet, the atmosphere is not friendly—nor relaxed. It seems that using this policy to get children to focus on eating is not really working.*

Objective *Develop and implement a lunchtime program that allows children to engage in social conversation but does not take the focus away from eating their lunch.*

Barriers *1) The current no-talking policy and 2) Current lunch schedule does not provide a mixed age group in the cafeteria at any one time.*

Stakeholders and Their Perspectives *Parents would have no objection to a program that helped children develop language as long as they were able to eat their lunch. Children just want to have fun, eat, and have more fun. Teachers do not object as long as it does not create a lot of extra work for them. The principal just wants a safe and productive lunchtime.*

Constituents	Allies	Opponents
Mary Martin, third-grade teacher *Jennifer Wooden, first-grade teacher* *Robert Hopkins, fifth-grade teacher*	*Most teachers are interested in possible plans*	*No one has posed strong objections*

Primary Targets for Advocacy	**Secondary Targets for Advocacy**
Principal	*Key teachers and key individuals in the PTA*

Long-Term Goals	**Short-Term Goals**
Develop a Lunch Families Plan	Research lunchroom policies from other schools
Initiate the plan, thus overriding no-talk recess policy	Research the importance of conversation in language development
	Talk to other teachers about their ideas
	Form an advocacy group
	Develop an initial plan for the Lunch Families Plan
	Present the plan to grade-level groups and refine based on their input
	Contact volunteer organization to see whether using the Foster Grandparent program would be feasible
	Present the plan to parent group for input and revise accordingly
	Develop a presentation for the principal
	Adjust plan based on principal's input
	Recruit and train volunteers
	Implement plan

Networks and Coalitions You Can Work With   School dietitians; Foster Grandparent group; Parent–Teacher Association; NAEYC, a local affiliate

Educational Tactics	**Persuasive Tactics**	**Mobilization Tactics**
Report on language development	PowerPoint Presentations	Form advocacy group
Report on lunchroom policies	Visit key stakeholders	Consult with dietitians
Create fact sheet		Host event

Timeline	
September 2006	Research lunchroom policies of other schools (Allison)
October 2006	Research the importance of conversation in language development (Allison)
October 2006	Talk to other teachers about their ideas (Allison)
October 2006	Form an advocacy group (Mary, Jennifer, Robert, and Allison)
December 2006	Develop an initial plan for the Lunch Families Plan (advocacy group)
January 2007	Present the plan to grade-level groups and refine based on their input; recruit new members to the advocacy group (Mary and Robert)

(continued)

Figure 8.8 *continued*

February 2007	Contact volunteer organization to see whether using the Foster Grandparent program would be feasible. Recruit new members for advocacy group (Dawn and Jennifer)
March 2007	Present plan to parent group for input and revise accordingly. Recruit new members of the advocacy group (advocacy group)
April 2007	Develop a presentation for the principal (Robert, Allison, Jonathan (a parent), and Kathleen (from the Foster Grandparent's Association)
April 2007	Adjust plan based on the principal's input (advocacy group)
June 2007	Recruit and train volunteers (Kathleen)
September 2007	Prepare and send out press release (Mary)
October 2007	Implement plan
November 2007	Fine-tune the plan based on operation and feedback from stakeholders (advocacy group)
December 2007	Host event to showcase Family Lunches. Invite all district principals and assistant principals, school board members, administrators of the Foster Grandparent program, and parents (school committee)
December 2007	Send thank-you notes to advocacy targets (Jane)

---

and mobilization tactics, and a flexible timeline. It may take many years to reach your ultimate goal. Effective advocacy strategies are flexible and must be revisited and revised often. It is important to stay motivated and avoid advocacy burnout. You can do this by celebrating small steps toward your goals.

RELEVANT CONCEPTS

network

advocacy group

collaborative discussion

synergistic melding

grassroots advocacy

coalitions

ad hoc coalitions

media contact list

press release

public service announcement

broadcast media

timeline

FOR FURTHER READING

The 7 Habits of Highly Effective People by Stephen R. Covey, 2004. Published by The Free Press.

Time Management from the Inside Out: The Foolproof Plan for Taking Control of Your Schedule and Your Life by Julie Morgenstein, 2004. Published by Henry Holt, Inc.

Remarkable Leadership: Unleashing Your Leadership Potential One Skill at a Time by Kevin Eikenberry and K. Eikenberry, 2007. Published by Jossey-Bass, Inc.

LINKS TO ADVOCACY RESOURCES

The following Web sites will give you tips for event planning, public speaking, and holding effective meetings.

Event Planning Tips

http://librarysupport.net/librarylovers/eventips.html

Event Planning Checklist

http://www.thegreatevent.com/content/ap.asp?id=4

Presentation Tips for Public Speaking

http://www.aresearchguide.com/3tips.html

How to Conduct Successful Business Meetings

http://www.altika.com/leadership/Meeting.htm

QUESTIONS FOR REFLECTION AND DISCUSSION

1. Compare your own professional network with other members of the class. How can you begin to expand this network?

2. Think about the last meeting you went to. Do you feel it was an effective meeting? Why or why not? Discuss how you could make the next meeting more effective.

3. Discuss your own experience or concerns about working with the media. Have you, or do you know of anyone whose words or actions have been misrepresented by news organizations? How can you prevent that from happening?

ADVOCACY IN ACTION: APPLICATION ACTIVITIES

1. Choose an issue that is relevant to infants, young children, or their families. This issue could be related to any of the contexts discussed in Chapter 2. There are many examples of such issues throughout the book. You could build on one of them. Develop an advocacy agenda using the worksheet provided in the Appendix.

2. Develop a network list of individuals and organizations in your area that work on issues related to infants, young children, and their families.

3. Create a PSA related to your advocacy issue.

4. Create a media list for your immediate area.

Part III Advocacy as Lifestyle

Chapter 9: Advocacy in the Global Community

CONNECTIONS

Thinking globally, what issues do you believe to be the most crucial to the well being of the world's children? What connections do you see between your habits as a consumer and the living conditions of children in your community or around the globe?

Profile of an Advocate

John Braxton is a second-grade teacher in a rural community near Youngstown, Ohio. As a father and teacher, he is concerned about the conditions of all the world's children, particularly as they relate to issues of social justice and equity. He continually works to understand the connections between these conditions, the policies of his own state and federal governments, and his actions as a teacher of young children, an informed voter, and a responsible consumer. John has become particularly concerned with the effects of global warming on climate change. These changes will ultimately affect economic conditions around the globe. He understands the devastating effect this will have on all the world's children. He now makes it a point to conserve energy in every way he can. He buys environmentally friendly products and systematically recycles used materials. John recently bought a hybrid car even though most days he carpools to work. He also studies the voting records of public officials and supports those that foster an environmentally friendly agenda.

Mr. Braxton's commitment to issues of social equity and the environment transcends his personal life and has become central to the classroom culture he creates with his students. Lessons about conservation of the environment's resources are integrated throughout both the curriculum and daily routines. His students understand and practice the principles of conflict resolution and they also interact with children from throughout the world via Internet pen pals. Globes and maps are much used tools in this classroom. Children often bring in news stories of both local and world events. As they share their stories they locate the countries discussed. In this informal way, they are developing global literacy.

His second-grade class planned and carried out a fund-raising event, donating the proceeds to HEIFER International to buy a flock of chickens and a heifer for a community in Africa. The student's chose this organization to receive their funds after they researched its track record and policies. They learned that HEIFER International practices a *pass it on* philosophy. That is, recipients of the livestock paid for by donors are required to donate the first offspring of this livestock to another community in need of an economic stimulus. John's students realized that this policy amplified the worth of their original donation.

John Braxton, by modeling a lifestyle committed to advocating for the well being of all the world's children, is teaching his students that there is a connection between all the world's citizens. More importantly, his students are learning that they can make a positive contribution to the world.

As you read the paper or listen to the news each morning, you hear of complex world issues such as extreme poverty, war and armed conflict, and global warming that affect children and families around the globe. You may have a tendency to believe that these issues are far away, much too complex for you to do anything about, and actually happening just to *them* and not to you or people you know. Such issues certainly are complex and resolutions do rely on high-level negotiation and diplomacy by world leaders. However, for many of the world's troublesome issues, there is a cause-and-effect cycle that often involves policies of our federal or state governments or of corporate industries that we do business with on a regular basis (Clinton, 2007). This fact brings these issues close to home and creates a connectedness to our own communities and to the families of the children we work with. It is because of this connectedness that early childhood educators, acting as global citizens, should become involved and advocate for positive changes for infants, children, and families throughout the world. The purpose of this chapter is to provide a brief overview of several global issues and describe ways that early childhood professionals can advocate to assure all children throughout the world have the opportunity to fulfill their greatest potential.

GLOBAL CITIZENSHIP

We live today in a **global society,** that is, a fast-changing and interdependent world in which policies and activities enacted in one part of the world affect the lives of citizens in all other parts of the world (Oxfam International, 2006). As early childhood professionals, we have an ethical responsibility to serve as a voice for young children everywhere (NAEYC, 2005). Therefore it is important to understand that there is a relationship between the immense problems that exist in some parts of the world and the policies that are created by governments and industries in other parts of the world (Bigelow & Peterson, 2002). Furthermore, resolutions to these complex problems require unified actions that can begin in our own communities.

> As we gain a greater appreciation for how life is connected around the globe, we understand better that what happens to a child in one part of the world affects others elsewhere. Our responsibility as child advocates spans borders not just between neighborhoods and states but from one country to another. Through collective efforts to speak out for children, we build a foundation for a more positive and peaceful world in which all children can live and thrive. (Lombardi, 2007, p. 11)

In this text, we will use the term **globalization** to imply that everyone in the world has some influence on everyone else, it may be either a positive or a negative influence, but there is an interdependence among all the citizens of the world (Bigelow & Peterson, 2002; Clinton, 2007). **Global citizens** are people who are aware of the wider world and have an understanding of how it works and feel a sense of **solidarity** with other citizens in the world (Bigelow & Peterson, 2002). Solidarity is not based on feelings of sympathy but on an understanding of common interests and connectedness. Global citizens respect and value diversity and are outraged by social injustice. They take responsibility for their actions and the actions of their governments and work, through a variety of contexts, to make the world a more equitable and sustainable place (Oxfam International, 2006). John Braxton is a global citizen. He works to understand the complexity of issues that affect children and families around the world and feels a sense of solidarity with them. He integrates advocacy strategies into his way of thinking, living, and being in the world, that is, these strategies have become a part of his lifestyle.

The worldwide early childhood professional community has an important role to play, both nationally and internationally, in putting pressure on governments to develop policies based on the needs and rights of children, thus giving them multiple opportunities to maximize their potential. In this way, early childhood advocates can transcend political processes and become vehicles for peace building (Connolly, Hayden, & Levin, 2007). What follows here is a brief overview, certainly oversimplified, of several interconnected issues that affect infants, children, and families around the world. The intent is not to give a detailed description of the issues, their cause, effects, or proposed solutions, but instead to offer resources useful in developing background knowledge and information about organizations and campaigns working to resolve these issues. We will frame the discussion of global issues with a description of human rights, specifically children's rights as put forth by the United Nations (UN).

HUMAN RIGHTS

Human rights are those rights which are essential to live as human beings. They represent the basic standards people need to be able to survive with dignity and hope. The UN created a common standard for human rights with the adoption of the Universal Declaration of Human Rights in 1948. This declaration is not part of a binding international law but provides a framework that recognizes that people of all races and religions are to be treated equally. Since 1948, six legally binding international **human rights instruments,** or treaties, have been adopted by the UN. They are

- International Covenant on Civil and Political Rights
- International Covenant on Economic, Social, and Cultural Rights
- Convention on the Rights of the Child
- Convention Against Torture and Other Cruel, Inhuman or Degrading Treatment or Punishment
- International Convention on the Elimination of All Forms of Racial Discrimination
- Convention of the Elimination of All Forms of Discrimination Against Women

The United Nations plays an important role in advocating for the needs of children and families across the globe.

Jacobs Stock Photography/Getty Images, Inc.—Photodisc

Every country in the world has ratified at least one of these treaties and they have become important tools for holding governments accountable for the protection of the rights of individuals in their countries.

The **Convention on the Rights of the Child** (United Nations, 1990) delineates the conditions that must be realized for children to develop their full potential. These conditions include freedom from hunger, neglect, and abuse. They also recognize that access to health care and education are rights for all children rather than a privilege for some. However, despite the existence of the Convention, children throughout the world, even in industrialized countries such as the United States, still suffer from extreme poverty, homelessness, abuse, neglect, preventable diseases, unequal access to education, and exposure to justice systems that do not recognize their special needs.

By ratifying the Convention, governments become obligated to create laws and policies that support the full implementation of the Convention.

This task is one that must be embraced not just through a government's declaration but through their actions and the actions of all members of society including families and service agencies and institutions. Therefore the advocacy activities of early childhood professionals throughout the world are essential for the realization of the Convention to occur on a global scale.

Grounded by the UN's Convention of the Rights of the Child, the global movement to promote early development has become a critical part of advocacy strategies aimed at fostering long-term health care, education, poverty reduction, and social protection for all the world's children.

> Globally, child and family advocates are working hard, standing up for the rights of children, making sure policy makers understand that learning begins at birth and promoting parent education, preschool programs, and education improvements in the early grades. (Lombardi, 2007, p. 10)

However, investment in early childhood development and education vary widely across nations and the world. Therefore, much work still needs to be done. Figure 9.1 provides resources to develop a better awareness about the plight of the world's children as it relates to children's rights. Figure 9.2 highlights advocacy groups and campaigns that are dedicated to fostering the rights of children and are active throughout the world.

EXTREME POVERTY

Extreme poverty (living on less than $1 a day) creates the situation where people cannot meet basic needs of survival such as food, water, clothing, sanitation, education, and health care (Sachs, 2005). The causes of extreme poverty are varied but include war, internal political conflict, government corruption, and displacement due to war or natural disasters. The consequences of extreme poverty include epidemic diseases such as AIDS, malaria, and tuberculosis; lack of opportunities for education; and conditions that bring forth sweatshops, child labor, and exploitations (Sachs, 2005). In many parts of the world including the United States, poverty passes through several generations.

Extreme poverty is most common in parts of Africa, Asia, and Central America, but it exists in every country of the world. The proportion of people in extreme poverty fell from 59% to 19% in the 20th century and

Figure 9.1 Internet Resources to Develop Awareness of Children's Rights

---

Clearinghouse on International Developments in Youth and Family Policies at Columbia University

www.childpolicyintl.org/

This site offers cross-cultural comparative information about programs, services, and benefits in 23 industrial nations.

Convention on the Rights of the Child

http://www.unicef.org/crc/index_30160.html or google "Convention on the Rights of the Child"

The Convention on the Rights of the Child is the first legally binding international instrument to incorporate the full range of human rights.

Global Action for Children

www.globalactionforchildren.org/ or google "Global Action for Children"

Provides resources and information on orphans and other vulnerable children in the developing world.

United Nations Educational, Scientific, and Cultural Organization (UNESCO)

www.unesco.org/

Provides an education portal that outlines policy briefs, global research, and case studies related to early childhood issues around the world.

World Association of Early Childhood Educators (WAECE)

www.waece.org/

Provides bilingual resources on a wide range of topics including peace education, child abuse prevention, and prenatal education.

World Bank Early Childhood Development

www.worldbanks.org/children

Provides links to international and regional partners, reports, journals, useful Web sites, and specific early childhood development resources, and international data and statistics.

Education for All (EFA) from UNESCO

www.efa.report.unesco.org/ or google "Education for All"

The Global Monitoring Report, which comes out each year, evaluates the world's commitment to providing education to all children, youth, and adults.

The Global Movement for Children (GMC)

www.gmfc.org/

This is a world-wide movement of organizations and people committed to uniting their efforts to build a world fit for children.

Figure 9.2 Advocacy Groups and Campaigns for Children's Rights

---

Global Campaign for Education
www.campaignforeducation.org/
Promotes education as a basic human right for children and adults worldwide.

Global Fund for Children
www.globalfundforchildren.org/
Provides grants to community-based organizations working with children who are vulnerable.

World Organization for Early Childhood Education's US National Committee (OMEP-USNC)
www.omep-usnc.org/
This organization assists efforts to improve early childhood education and supports scientific research that influences conditions for optimal well-being.

Save the Children
www.savethechildren.org/
This organization works to create change for children in need around the world.

United Nations Children's Fund (UNICEF)
www.unicef.org/earlychildhood/index.html
This organization works for children's rights and provides resources for teachers and students on programs and current events.

International Institute for Child Rights and Development
http://web.uvic.ca/iicrd/ or google "International Institute for Child Rights and Development"
This is an international initiative, endorsed by the United Nations Committee on the Rights of the Child and the Office of the United Nations High Commissioner for Human Rights, to develop educational programs on the human rights of children for professionals working with and for children.

---

many economists believe that, with the collaborative effort of all governments, it can be eradicated by 2025 (Sachs, 2005). The UN's Millennium Development Goals, adopted in 2000, strive to meet the needs of the world's poorest citizens. These goals are

- Eradicate extreme poverty and hunger.
- Achieve universal primary education.
- Promote gender equality and empower women.
- Reduce child mortality.
- Improve maternal health.
- Combat HIV/AIDS, malaria, and other diseases.

Advocacy efforts are necessary in order to eliminate extreme poverty and provide educational opportunities for all children across the globe.

- Ensure environmental sustainability.
- Develop a global partnership for economic development.

The Millennium Villages Project is one campaign that strives to meet the millennium goals by providing an integrated approach to rural development. It is funded by cost-sharing partnerships between local, national, and international governments, innovative **nongovernment organizations (NGOs),** and universities.

> By improving access to clean water, sanitation and other essential infrastructure, education, food production, basic health care, and environmental sustainability, Millennium Villages ensures that communities living in extreme poverty have a real, sustainable opportunity to lift themselves out of the poverty trap. (Friedrich, 2007, pp. 1849–1851)

Debt relief is a poverty reducing strategy that requires international cooperation. The world's poorest countries often spend billions of dollars to repay loans made by wealthy nations and international institutions.

This leaves little for the development of basic infrastructures, health programs, and education. In 1990, development agencies, trade unions, university students, and churches came together to advocate for debt relief. They recruited the internationally known celebrity Bono to act as spokesperson for their campaign. As a result of this activism, a group of powerful nations cancelled 100% of the debt of 18 of the world's poorest countries. One of those countries, Uganda, used the money that would have gone to debt repayment to improve primary education and HIV/AIDS treatment (Cheadle & Prendergast, 2007).

Other poverty reduction strategies include the promotion of free trade among nations, direct aid to those living in poverty, and improving the social environments and economic skills of people through education. These strategies require **political will** and cooperation among local, national, and international governments. Political will is developed when advocates, including those in the early childhood community, from all nations unite to bring pressure on their elected leaders to act on behalf of the world's poorest children. Figure 9.3 provides resources to develop a better awareness about the plight of the world's children as it relates to living in extreme poverty. Figure 9.4 highlights advocacy groups and campaigns that are dedicated to fostering the elimination of extreme poverty for children throughout the world.

WAR AND ARMED CONFLICT

War and armed conflicts in today's society have a great impact on the lives of infants and children. Whole communities suffer from the loss of public services including access to education and health care. In addition, children are at risk of being separated from their families and become vulnerable to abduction by enemy factions, indoctrination into the lifestyle of child soldiers, and/or victimization through child slavery, rape, or sexual assault (Cheadle & Prendergast, 2007).

It is important to understand that the effects of living in the shadow of continual violence is not confined to foreign countries but exists in all societies across the world. The gang violence that exists in many urban areas of the United States creates the same kind of chaos in the lives of children as wars and civil unrests do elsewhere (Connolly et al., 2007). Children that live in the shadow of consistent violence often bear witness to crime and suffer from posttraumatic stress syndrome. This can result in changes to

Figure 9.3 Information on the Effects of Extreme Poverty

Books

The End of Poverty: Economic Possibilities for Our Time by Jeffrey D. Sachs, 2005. Published by Penguin Books.

Artisans of Democracy: How Ordinary People, Families in Extreme Poverty, and Social Institutions Become Allies to Overcome Social Exclusion by Jona M. Rosenfeld and Bruno Tardieu, 2000. Published by University Press of America.

Participatory Approaches to Attacking Extreme Poverty by Quentin Wodon, Xavier Godinot (Eds.), 2006. Published by World Bank Publications.

UN Millennium Development Goals

http://www.un.org/millenniumgoals/

Outlines the eight millennium development goals that form a blueprint agreed to by all the world's countries. They have galvanized unprecedented efforts to meet the needs of the world's poorest.

The World Health Organization

www.who.org/

The World Health Organization is the directing and coordinating authority for health within the United Nations system. It is responsible for providing leadership on global health matters, shaping the health research agenda, setting norms and standards, articulating evidence-based policy options, providing technical support to countries, and monitoring and assessing health trends.

---

their personality or temperament. They may suffer reoccurring nightmares, sleep disorders, excessive attachment or loss of attachment to significant adults, withdrawal, and/or depression (Connolly et al., 2007). In addition, living with continued violence may lead to emotional difficulties such as a deep sense of anxiety and insecurity, low self-esteem, or delays in moral or social development (Connolly et al., 2007).

Resolving wars and conflicts throughout the world is a complex task that needs local, federal, and international attention. Early childhood professionals can begin advocacy for world peace in their own communities and in their schools (1) by raising the awareness of the issues among their neighbors and colleagues, (2) by practicing ethical consumerism, (3) by advocating for disinvestment of government funds, and finally by helping to develop the political will to resolve worldwide conflicts through informed voting in federal, state, and local elections. An explanation of these basic advocacy strategies will be developed later in this chapter.

Figure 9.4 Groups and Campaigns Dedicated to the Elimination of Poverty

RESULTS
http://www.results.org/
This is a nonprofit grassroots organization committed to creating political will to end hunger and the worst aspects of poverty. Includes a link to the Education for All campaign.

HEIFER International
http://www.heifer.org/
This nonprofit international organization is dedicated to ending generations of poverty by providing communities with livestock to help them develop a sustainable economy. The Web site offers ideas for education and fund-raising projects that can be undertaken by individuals or groups such as classrooms of children.

Doctors without Borders
http://www.doctorswithoutborders.org/
Doctors without Borders is an independent international medical organization that delivers emergency aid to people affected by armed conflict, epidemics, natural or man-made disasters, or exclusion from health care.

Global Fairness Initiative
http://www.globalfairness.org/
The Global Fairness Initiative is founded on the premise that economic globalization should work to improve the lives of impoverished and marginalized populations around the world by creating economic opportunities.

People & Planet
http://www.peopleandplanet.org/
This organization promotes activism on the part of college students by sponsoring campaigns in the areas of economic justice, HIV/AIDS, and climate change.

Figure 9.5 provides resources to develop a better awareness about the effects of violence, war, and armed conflict on the world's children. Figure 9.6 highlights advocacy groups and campaigns that are dedicated to fostering peaceful communities for children throughout the world.

GLOBAL WARMING

Global warming refers to the increase in the average temperature of the Earth's near-surface air and oceans that has occurred in recent decades. Although a full explanation of global warming and its consequences is

Figure 9.5 Resources for Understanding the Effects of Violence, War, and Armed Conflict

---

Books

From Conflict to Peace Building: The Power of Early Childhood Initiatives: Lessons from Around the World by Paul Connolly and Jacqueline Hayden with Diane Levin, 2007. Published by World Forum Foundation.

Free the Children: A Young Man Fights Against Child Labor and Proves That Children Can Change the World by Craig Kielburger with Kevin Major, 1998. Published by Harper Perennial.

Not on Our Watch: The Mission to End Genocide in Darfur and Beyond by Don Cheadle and John Prendergast, 2007. Published by Hyperion.

The Enemy Has a Face: The Seeds of Peace Experience by John Wallach and Michael Wallach, 2006. Published by United States Institute of Peace Press.

Zlata's Diary: A Child's Life in Wartime Sarajevo by Zlata Filipovic, 2006. Published by Penguin Group. (Adolescent Literature)

A Long Way Gone: Memoirs of a Boy Soldier by Ishmael Beah, 2007. Published by HarperCollins. (Adolescent Literature)

Breadwinner by Deborah Ellis, 2001. Published by Oxford University Press. (Adolescent Literature)

---

beyond the scope of this chapter, we can summarize its effects by describing a cycle of activities that starts with the unlimited burning of fossil fuels, such as oil, coal, and natural gas. This causes a **greenhouse effect** that results in a gradual increase in the temperature of the earth's atmosphere. This increase in temperature may cause climatic changes across the globe which in turn may cause increased storm activity, more frequent and severe droughts, the proliferation of harmful insects, and the dying-off of food sources. If these events occur, large groups of people may be displaced from their homes, which could lead to a rise in the poverty rate or even violence when one group of people invades the territory of another group of people (Knauer, 2007).

Even though there has been intense social and political debate about the possible effects of global warming, scientists throughout the world have been working for several decades to bring international action to slow the process. The primary international agreement on combating global warming is the Kyoto Protocol, an amendment to the United Nations Framework Convention on Climate Change (UNFCCC) negotiated

Figure 9.6 Advocacy Groups and Campaigns for World Peace

International Working Group on Peace Building with Young Children

www.peacebuildingwithyoungchildren.org/

This working group is a global initiative by early childhood practitioners, researchers, and civil society organizations to make visible the role of early childhood development as a force for reconciliation and peace building in regions experiencing or emerging from armed conflicts.

PeacePlayers International

www.playingforpeace.org/

PeacePlayers International is a global organization that uses sport to unite and educate young people in divided communities. It was founded on the premise that "children who play together can learn to live together."

Seeds of Peace

www.seedsofpeace.org/

This organization is dedicated to empowering young leaders from regions of conflict. It provides an international model for the development of leadership skills necessary to advance reconciliation and coexistence.

Vital Voices Democracy Initiative

www.vitalvoices.org/

Vital Voices Global Partnership invests in emerging women leaders by providing education and support to build leadership capacity in areas of economic development, political participation, and human rights.

Pennies for Peace

www.penniesforpeace.org/

Pennies for Peace educates American children about the world beyond their experience and shows them they can make a positive impact on a global scale, one penny at a time.

---

in 1997. As of October, 2007, the United States had not ratified this treaty, claiming that it would create serious harm to the U.S. economy. Many activist groups have been formed to educate the public of possible threats to all societies and to create the political will to implement solutions. Early childhood professionals can join ongoing campaigns to bring about awareness and real solutions to the environment issues that face the earth. Figure 9.7 provides resources to develop a better awareness of the causes and effects of global warming on the earth. Figure 9.8 highlights advocacy groups and campaigns that are dedicated to finding and implementing solutions to global warming.

Figure 9.7 Resources for Understanding Global Warming

Books

Global Warming: The Causes; The Perils; The Solutions; The Actions: What You Can Do by Kelly Knauer (Ed.) 2007. Published by Time Inc: Home Entertainment.

An Inconvenient Truth: The Crisis of Global Warming by Al Gore (2007). Published by Penguin Young Readers Group.

Cool It: The Skeptical Environmentalists Guide to Global Warming by Bjorn Lomborg, 2007. Published by Knopf Publishing.

Last Child in the Woods: Saving Our Children from Nature-Deficit Disorder by Richard Louv, 2006. Published by Algonquin Books of Chapel Hill.

Rescuing a Planet Under Stress and a Civilization in Trouble by Lester R. Brown, 2006. Published by W.W. Norton.

Pew Center on Global Climate Change

www.pewclimate.org/

The Pew Center on Global Climate Change brings together business leaders, policy makers, scientists, and other experts to bring a new approach to the complex and controversial issue of climate change.

STRATEGIES FOR GLOBAL ADVOCACY

The strategies used for advocacy in the global community are not different from the strategies used in other contexts and have been described in detail throughout this text. However, acts of global advocacy often take the form

Figure 9.8 Advocacy Groups and Campaigns for Solutions to Global Warming

---

Global Green USA

http://www.globalgreen.org/

This is an international environmental organization that addresses three of the greatest challenges facing humanity: stemming global climate change; eliminating weapons of mass destruction; and providing clean, safe drinking water for all people.

National Green Pages

http://www.coopamerica.org/pubs/greenpages/index.cfm

The National Green Pages is a directory listing nearly 3000 businesses that have made firm commitments to sustainable, socially just principles, including the support of sweatshop-free labor, organic farms, fair trade, and cruelty-free products.

---

of personal commitments that result in lifestyle changes. For example, you may be committed to conserving the environment and slowing global warming. This commitment may result in downsizing your living space, recycling your wastes, or driving an energy-efficient hybrid vehicle. Early childhood professionals who make a commitment to advocate for children's rights and world peace may develop and implement curricula and management strategies that foster **global literacy,** that is, an understanding of the interconnectedness of the world and its people. They may also introduce conflict resolution strategies that foster peaceful classrooms. Their actions model the dispositions and strategies children will need to learn in order to meet the challenges they will confront as they grow up to be productive global citizens (Oxfam International, 2006).

In making these lifestyle changes, global citizens become what Cheadle and Prendergast (2007) refer to as *upstanders*. **Upstanders,** in contrast to bystanders, take action instead of just watching or assuming that others will take action to foster a more just world. What follows here is a review of advocacy strategies framed in a global context.

Raising Awareness

It takes time and thought to develop a true understanding of the complex issues such as poverty or global warming. It is important to reason and think through issues and solutions for yourself and not just accept the opinions of those you know or those that hold the power in your community. Reading books, particularly books that objectively present the history of issues chronologically, will help develop a true understanding. Reading newspaper and journal articles and information posted on Web sites will provide multiple perspectives on any issue or proposed solutions.

Another way to raise your awareness as it relates to a particular issue is to join or form discussion groups with friends, colleagues, or other interested members of your community. Group meetings can be devoted to reviewing reading material, discussing different viewpoints related to issues and solutions, drawing connections with policies and practices taking place in your country or community, and/or developing advocacy strategies. Figure 9.9 describes the action steps involved in forming an Awareness-Raising Discussion group.

Figure 9.9 Forming an Awareness-Raising Discussion Group

1. Select an issue that affects children and families around the world, for example, health care, early education, or growing up in the shadow of violence.

2. Do a preliminary search for books, articles, and Internet resources related to the topic. Choose two or three selections to send to the members of your group. Make sure your selections include a variety of opinions on the topic and anecdotes that describe the effect of your issue on children across the world.

3. Set the date, time, and location of the first group meeting and send invitations to friends and colleagues. Explain that the purpose of the group is to develop a better understanding of factors that face children in today's world. Send the reading list with the invitation and ask guests to research the topic on their own and bring additional material to the first meeting.

4. At the first meeting, have everyone share their reaction to the materials they have read. Discuss how the issue affects children in your own community as well as children around the world.

5. Decide as a group what your next steps might be. Members may choose to study the issue more by researching specific aspects of the issue or by inviting a speaker to attend the next meeting.

6. Eventually, the group may want to reach out to the broader community in an effort to bring further public awareness to this issue. This could be done through letters to the editor, speaking at community meetings, or sponsoring a public event.

Networking

Joining forces with others is the most effective way early childhood professionals can effect world change. Each of us must do our part, but we do not have to do it alone. There are many ongoing campaigns that can be accessed via Internet sites: campaigns to foster social equity and fair trade across the globe, campaigns to ratify the Convention of the Rights of the Child, and campaigns to slow global warming and preserve the ecology of the earth. Examples of these have been presented throughout this chapter.

Joining a professional organization that has an agenda for world advocacy can help individuals connect with others who have similar interests. The Association for Childhood Education International (ACEI) provides a vehicle for individuals to work together to support global results for children.

See their Web site at http://acei.org/advocacy.htm for resources and links to other like-minded groups. Also, the National Association for the Education of Young Children offers valuable resources that support their commitment to children and excellence in early education through their Global Alliance for the Education of Young Children (www.naeyc.org/globalalliance).

Informed Voting

As with all advocacy issues, being an informed voter is a crucial aspect of action. Political will is needed to resolve the complex issues that face children and families. Informal voters who press candidates to discuss their positions on critical issues keep these issues in the news and in the minds of other voters, thus creating the political will needed to effect change. Environmental and social justice issues relate to elections at all levels of government. For example, any government officials, from a school board member to the president of the United States, will be involved in awarding multimillion-dollar contracts for goods and services. It is important to learn a candidate's position as it relates to dealing with companies or governments who have a known record of unethical behavior on human rights governmental issues. Candidates for Congress or the presidency should be asked to articulate their policy regarding such things as debt relief for developing countries, reduction of carbon emissions, fair trade agreements, and the ratification of the Convention on the Rights of the Child.

It is also important to hold elected officials accountable for their campaign promises. By maintaining vigilance over elected officials' policy development and voting records and making sure that this information gets into the hands of the electorate, advocates can affect political will and have a positive impact on the global community.

Ethical Consumerism

Ethical consumerism is the act of choosing what you buy based on what you know about the ethical practices used by the manufacturer or retailer of the product. In other words, you begin to *think globally but act locally*. There are two forms of ethical consumerism: **positive buying** and the **moral boycott.** When practicing positive buying, you consider the people who make the things you buy. You wonder about the conditions they work in and what they are paid. You research the companies that you buy from to find out if their labor, trade, and environmental policies foster world issues such as extreme poverty or global warming. You choose products that have been created and marketed under conditions that promote fair trade and environmental stability (Bigelow & Peterson, 2002).

When you learn that companies violate principles of social justice and equity, or employ practices that harm the environment, you engage in a moral boycott and enlist the support of others. There is evidence that moral boycotts by consumers do create change of practices even among the world's largest and most powerful corporations. Wal-Mart, a company that operates in 14 different countries, came under fire by consumer and activist groups in the early 1990s for many of its polices including its lack of attention to environmental conservation. They have now instituted the Sustainability 360 plan that has three goals: (1) to be supplied 100% by renewable energy, (2) to create zero waste, and (3) to sell sustainable products that conserve resources and protect the environment (Clinton, 2007).

Consumers can discover the ethical practices of leading industries through Internet searches. One Web site, Responsible Shopper, reports on information regarding the impact of major corporations on human rights, social justice, and environmental impact. The National Green Pages (see Figure 9.8) is a directory that lists businesses that have made commitments to operate under principles that foster social justice throughout the world and support the world's environment. Both sites can be accessed from Co-op America (http://www.coopamerica.org).

Labels on products can also lead consumers to products created under humane conditions and marketed using fair labor practices. For example, the Market for Fair Trade Coffee is an NGO. Companies that will ensure that their coffee farmers earn a decent income are invited to join. Coffees produced by these companies get to display the Fair Trade Coffee label. Labels can also indicate if a product is made of recycled material or if it is itself recyclable.

Disinvestment

Disinvestment, which also is referred to as divestment, is the reduction of some kind of asset in order to pressure a government, industry, or company to change its policy (Cheadle & Prendergast, 2007). In most cases, stocks in corporations are sold, resulting in a lower overall market value for the company. This initial disinvestment may encourage others to sell their stocks out of fear of loss of revenue. Eventually the corporation will lose its power to raise funds or expand business.

The term was first used in the 1980s to describe the economic boycott that pressured the government of South Africa to abolish its policy of apartheid. Initially the disinvestment movement was spearheaded by college students with support from human rights, labor, and civil rights leaders. In 1986, Congress passed the Anti-Apartheid Act that blocked the import of South American products and prevented new corporate investments. "This economic pressure generated by American citizens helped to force the South African government to change its ways. Mandela was released from prison in Feb. 1990 and elected president of South Africa in 1994—the apartheid era was over" (Cheadle & Prendergast, 2007, p. 107).

Not everyone agrees with disinvestment strategies, but they are worth considering because, when you join ranks with others, a powerful statement can be made and pressure can be put on corporations or governments to enact more humane and environmentally friendly policies. As an advocate for children's rights and social justice, you can join networks that advocate for disinvestment at your university, place of employment, or agencies of your state government.

Fund-Raising/Charitable Giving

Fund-raising and charitable giving are an important part of all advocacy activities because money is needed to get the message out about issues that are important to young children. Money is also important when creating model projects that support the development of the potential of all the world's children. However, it is important to understand where the funds you raise or donate are going and how they are to be used. Before donating funds to an advocacy group, investigate the history of the group as well as their track record related to accomplishing the goals they set forward. This is what the children in John Braxton's classroom did before they chose HEIFER International as the recipient for their fund-raising efforts. They made this choice because HEIFER uses the "pass it on principle."

There are many well-established groups that maximize the effects of even the most modest contributions of individuals. Kiva is an NGO that offers individual investors the opportunity to choose who will receive their funds. The contributor can log onto the Kiva Web site and read prescreened grant requests posted by individuals from all over the world. The contributor then chooses a recipient and sends funds to Kiva via the use of a credit card. Kiva combines all donations for each proposal and works with lenders in the recipients' home community to make the final transfer of funds. This transaction model brings economic benefits to the whole community.

Another organization that has a proven track record in using funds to the betterment of entire communities is World Bicycle Relief. This organization was founded in 2005 by SRAM Corporation and Trek Bicycle in response to the 2004 tsunami that swept the Indian Ocean. The project has since expanded across the globe. Donated bicycles are used for a variety of purposes including transportation to and from work or for health care workers to visit patients. Figure 9.10 provides contact information for Kiva, World Bicycle Relief, and other NGOs that collect funds and redistribute them to individuals and communities.

Money alone will not solve the complex problems that face the children of the world. Therefore, policy advocacy should go hand in hand with fund-raising. It is government policies and cooperation between governments that will support long-term solutions that lead to an equitable and just world for all. Policies will be changed as citizens of the world become more aware and more active. For example, UNICEF raises approximately $90 million a year, but this amount will never fund all the projects that are needed to make a just world. It is people putting pressure on governments and corporations that will make the biggest difference in the world (Bigelow & Peterson, 2002).

SUMMARY

In today's global society, policies and activities enacted in one part of the world affect the lives of citizens around the world. The early childhood professional community can play an important role in transcending the political process and work to ensure that basic human rights for all children are realized and that the effects of global warming are slowed down. Advocacy strategies in the global arena are not different from strategies in other arenas but often develop into lifestyle choices. These strategies include maintaining a high awareness of issues and their connectiveness

Figure 9.10 Funding Organizations

HEIFER International
www.heifer.org/
This organization helps individuals buy livestock for communities in need in order to develop long-term economic sustainability.

Kiva
www.kiva.org/
Kiva lets individuals connect with and loan money to unique small businesses in the developing world.

Oprah's Angel Network
www.oprahsangelnetwork.org/
This is a public charity that awards grants to organizations operating projects that make a difference in underserved communities.

Challah for Hunger
www.challahforhunger.org
This is a national student organization that addresses humanitarian issues by selling loaves of Challah and donating the money to projects that support the development of social justice around the world.

Bill and Melinda Gates Foundation
www.gatesfoundation.org
This is a public charity that awards grants for global development, education, and health initiatives.

World Bicycle Relief
www.worldbicyclerelief.org/
This organization partners with relief agencies to provide quality bicycles to people who need them to improve their lives through education or access to economic opportunities.

eBay Giving Works
http://givingworks.ebay.com/
Through this Web site, eBay provides a way to donate all or part of the final sale price of an item you list to a nonprofit organization you choose. eBay then collects and distributes the funds and sends you a tax receipt.

Share Your Soles
http://www.shareyoursoles.org
This organization collects donations and "gently worn shoes" and distributes them to those in greatest need.

---

to policies created by your own government representatives, networking with others and taking part in global campaigns, being an informed voter, and practicing ethical consumerism. Early childhood professionals can also affect children around the world by monitoring their investments and the investment practices of their employers and state governments. Fundraising and charitable giving can also support the implementation of global policies that will positively affect our world and its environment.

RELEVANT CONCEPTS

global society

globalization

global citizen

solidarity

human rights

human rights instruments

Convention on the Rights of the Child

extreme poverty

nongovernment organization (NGO)

debt relief

political will

global warming

greenhouse effect

global literacy

upstanders

ethical consumerism

positive buying

moral boycott

disinvestment

FOR FURTHER READING

High Noon: Twenty Global Problems: Twenty Years to Solve Them by J. F. Richard, 2002. Published by Basic Books.

If the World Were a Village: A Book about the World's People by David J. Smith and illustrated by Shelagh Armstrong, 2002. Published by Kids Can Press.

Ghosts from the Nursery: Tracing the Roots of Violence by Robin Karr-Morse and
   Meredith S. Wiley, 1997. Published by The Atlantic Monthly Press.
A Kid's Guide to Giving by Freddi Zeiler, 2006. Published by Innovative Kids.

LINKS TO ADVOCACY RESOURCES

UNICEF: Child Rights

http://unicef.org/crc/

Provides information and publication on the work of the United Nations Children's Fund and its advocacy for children's rights, survival, development, and protection through adoption of the Convention of the Rights of the Child.

The National Center for Children in Poverty

http://www.nccp.org/

Produces reports, fact sheets, and press material that highlight strategies to end child poverty in the United States.

QUESTIONS FOR REFLECTION AND DISCUSSION

1. Would you consider yourself a global citizen? In what ways are you? What actions could you take to increase your effectiveness as a global citizen?

2. Reflect on your habits as a consumer and discuss possible effects of your current lifestyle on children around the world.

3. What can you do immediately to contribute to the health and well being of children in a developing country? What can you do within the next five years?

4. In the Profile of an Advocate, John Braxton is described as being concerned about issues related to social justice and equality. Yet much of his personal advocacy agenda concerns global warming. Discuss the connection between these two important issues.

ADVOCACY IN ACTION: APPLICATION ACTIVITIES

1. Go through your closet or your pantry and make a list of the companies you buy from. Review the Web site www.coopamerica.org/programs/rs/. Locate information on a corporation that sells products that you consume regularly. Check their history as it relates to environmental and human rights issues. Also note if there are any campaigns to encourage changes in their policies. Report on your findings and reflect on how this new information will change your spending habits.

2. Plan an Awareness Raising Discussion Group (see Figure 9.9, Forming an Awareness-Raising Discussion Group). What issue will you choose? Who would you like to come? What reading materials would you like to send to the group ahead of time? What would be your outcome goals?

3. There are several charitable organizations listed in Figure 9.10 that work on an international scale. Choose three of these NGOs (or find one or two on your own) and research their history, mission, policies for distributing funds, and track record as successful change agents. Compare and contrast these agencies and explain which you would rather contribute to and why.

Chapter 10: Volunteerism as Advocacy

CONNECTIONS

When have you done volunteer work? What kind of work was it? Why did you get involved? What knowledge and skills did you gain from the work? How did it benefit others?

Profile of an Advocate

Amanda Redford is a kindergarten teacher in Rochester, New York. She also volunteers with children who have been abused or neglected as a court-appointed special advocate (CASA). CASA volunteers are trained citizens appointed by a judge to represent the best interest of children whose home placement is being determined in juvenile court.

Amanda generally works on one case at a time. It can take several months or even a year to resolve the issues involved. During this time, she explores all placement options for the child and interviews all concerned parties. Throughout the process, she acts as an advocate for the child, helping him understand why he is in court and the roles the judges, lawyers, and social workers play. Amanda works to develop a trusting relationship with the child and encourages him to express feelings and opinions. She appears in court to report findings and make recommendations regarding placement.

Amanda first learned about CASA when she was interviewed by another CASA volunteer who was assigned to a case involving a student in Amanda's classroom. She reports that cases she works on are often difficult and time consuming, but the training she receives through the CASA organization and her direct experience with children and families has given her valuable insight into the court system and into issues related to neglected or abused children and their families. She has adjusted to the demanding schedule and made volunteerism a part of her lifestyle.

Amanda's volunteer work has not only taught her how important it is to advocate for the needs of children and families but also given her skills she needs to be effective. She is frequently asked to testify before the legislature regarding issues and policies that affect neglected or abused children. She has also gained a valuable network she can call upon when needed to influence policy decisions in her community and state. She is one person who, through her job and volunteer work, is truly making a difference for children and families in her community.

Volunteers are people who donate their time and energy to help individuals, organizations, and causes without expectation of monetary reward. Advocacy itself, taking on the challenge and responsibility for a cause without any promise or thought of financial gain, is a form of volunteerism. By working as volunteers for organizations and agencies that serve the best interests of infants, children, and families, early childhood professionals help shape the world around them rather than letting it shape them.

Volunteers plan, organize, and deliver an enormous range of services in our communities and in the process advocate for the well-being of young children and their families. In this chapter, we will discuss various aspects of volunteering and explore how early childhood professionals can gain knowledge, experience, and skills while serving children and families in their communities through volunteerism.

VOLUNTEERISM AS ADVOCACY

When early childhood professionals volunteer with agencies that support children and families, they gain valuable knowledge about the conditions children and families live in and the needs of service agencies. This gives them the credibility needed to be effective when speaking to others in the community and to policy makers.

People volunteer for a wide variety of reasons. Often it is because someone close to them had been positively affected by the work of a volunteer or service-oriented agency. Other reasons include the following: the satisfaction that comes from providing a needed service, helping solve a community problem, learning new skills, building a valuable network and promoting a cause they passionately believe in. Through volunteer service, you see firsthand the effect, both positive and negative, of agency and government policies on young children and their families. This knowledge and experience makes you a stronger advocate and puts you in touch with other like-minded professionals. The following scenario illustrates some of the benefits of volunteerism for students and professionals in the field of early childhood.

Janelle, an undergraduate in early childhood education, volunteers three hours a week at the Ronald McDonald House in her community. The Ronald McDonald House Charities is a nonprofit organization that provides "a home away from home" for families of seriously ill children receiving treatment at nearby hospitals. During the time Janelle works at the house she does a variety of tasks. Sometimes she entertains siblings of the children that are hospitalized. She may play with them, help them with their homework, or read them stories. Other times, Janelle cooks, packages, and stores meals in the house's community kitchen so that families can have something hearty and nutritious to eat when they return from the hospital. And sometimes, Janelle spends her time on office tasks related to fundraising. She enjoys all the tasks she does and has developed many new skills and the confidence that she can make a difference in the life of a child.

Because of her direct service at the house, she feels like an "insider" when it comes to understanding the issues that face families with children who have chronic illnesses. She has heard them speak of their issues and problems. She knows the effects that not having health insurance has on families. She has a stronger understanding for the need of universal health care and can speak to others from a standpoint of information rather than just principle or emotion.

Janelle has come to know the director of the house and many who are on the board, as well as fellow volunteers. They serve as models and mentors for her. She sees how tirelessly they work for a cause they believe in and this fosters her disposition to be an advocate. Although Janelle intends to continue her education leading to certification and earn a teaching certificate in early childhood, she is considering studying for a master's degree in child life service and working with chronically ill children and their families in the future.

Figure 10.1 sums up benefits for early childhood professionals who act as volunteers in their communities.

NONPROFIT ORGANIZATIONS

There are a vast number of not-for-profit (nonprofit) organizations in the United States and throughout the world whose missions are either service oriented, that is to provide human services to communities, or advocacy

Figure 10.1 Reasons to Volunteer

1. To demonstrate commitment to a cause or belief
2. To enrich the community you live in
3. To become an insider and learn firsthand about issues and problems facing children and families
4. To develop networks with other professionals
5. To share skills
6. To discover skills you didn't know you had
7. To gain new skills
8. To explore a career path
9. To receive mentoring from professionals
10. To foster the development of young children and their families

oriented, to advocate for social change. Examples of nonprofit organizations include food banks, child care centers, health care clinics, civil rights groups, environmental groups, educational institutions, children's museums, eye clinics, immunization clinics, and faith-based organizations.

Not-for-profit organizations exist to serve and promote the common good. But in doing so, they also create an opportunity for individuals to engage in advocacy and become actively involved in civic life (Alvarado, 2003). In fact, nonprofits rely heavily on volunteers to provide much-needed man power and resources in a time when many agencies are constantly adjusting to both budget cutbacks and a growing demand for service.

Service-Oriented Nonprofits

Some nonprofit groups focus primarily on providing resources and service to the community but also have an important advocacy agenda. The Ronald McDonald House Foundation, mentioned in the scenario above, is one example of a service-oriented not-for-profit organization. Other examples are The Young Men's Christian Association (YMCA) and the Young Women's Christian Association (YWCA). YMCAs are the largest not-for-profit community service organization in America. Since their founding, YMCAs have provided health and fitness programs as an integral part of their mission. As a part of their advocacy agenda they often provide human services such as child care, teen leadership and sports clubs, after-school programs, job training, new immigrant education, and parenting classes. Each association is different, reflecting the needs of the local community. Because they are a nonprofit organization, fees for services are generally low or on a sliding scale. This means that cost of a service is figured relative to each individual client's ability to pay. Funding for nonprofit agencies come from many sources including private foundations, community fund drives like the United Way, and federal and/or state appropriated funds.

In addition to providing services, many nonprofit organizations sustain an advocacy agenda aimed at public education relative to their mission. Volunteers become informed advocates and can influence policy makers on important issues. For example, the public often perceives that if a service exists it is available to all who need it. In many areas, programs are underfunded and cannot meet the needs of the community. Volunteers become acutely aware of this need and are then able to advocate for increases in funding.

Figure 10.2 provides Web site information for national service-oriented nonprofit organizations that may operate volunteer programs in most communities. There will be many other nonprofit service organizations operating in your community. These organizations include family service associations, community action programs, early intervention programs, and child care information and referral centers. You can find contact information for these and other agencies in your local phone book.

Advocacy-Oriented Nonprofits

The central mission of advocacy-oriented nonprofits is to impact public thinking and in turn public policy. They develop advocacy campaigns and lobby Congress to enact responsible policy. One example is the Children's Defense Fund. This advocacy organization works to ensure that America's underserved children have a healthy start in life. Another example of an advocacy-oriented nonprofit organization is the Parents Television Council (PTC). PTC campaigns to bring about responsive and responsible television programming for children and families. Figure 10.3 provides Web site information for other nonprofit, advocacy-oriented organizations that function to improve conditions for young children and families.

By connecting people, inspiring altruism, and giving a voice to local and far-reaching concerns, nonprofits, no matter what their mission, create connections that bind communities together (Alvarado, 2003). In the current economic climate, many not-for-profit organizations find themselves

Figure 10.2 Service-Oriented Nonprofits

Ronald McDonald House Charities
http://www.rmhc.com
RMHC supports three programs that directly improve the health and well-being
of children: The Ronald McDonald House, The Ronald McDonald Family Room,
and The Ronald McDonald Care Mobile.

The Young Men's Christian Organization
http://www.ymca.net
The YMCA is the largest not-for-profit community service organization in the
United States. It also operates in more than 120 countries. From child care to
programs for older adults, YMCA offers opportunities for individuals and families to grow in spirit, mind, and body at every stage of life.

National Court Appointed Special Advocate Association
http://www.nationalcasa.org
The national office of CASA works with state and local CASA volunteer groups
to promote and support quality volunteer advocacy to help assure each child a
safe, permanent, nurturing home.

Wings for Children
http://wingsforchildren.org
Wings for Children monitors state agencies charged with bringing better services for children. The Angel Wings program provides free air transportation to
and from various countries and states for children of abuse, neglect, exploitation and for children who have been stolen. Wings also provides transportation
for children that need medical treatment.

Jumpstart
http://jstart.org
Jumpstart works to engage caring, civic-minded college students in service to
work toward the day every child in America enters school prepared to succeed.

having to do more with fewer resources. In making each dollar go further,
the value of the volunteer is integral to maintaining a high level of service
to the community.

TYPES OF VOLUNTEER EFFORTS

There are many ways to support young children and families through volunteerism and in the process advocate for important issues. Volunteer
opportunities can be random and episodic in nature, or they can be long-
term, consistent commitments. Participants can volunteer as individuals,

Figure 10.3 Advocacy-Oriented Nonprofits

Children's Defense Fund
http://www.childrensdefense.org/site/pageserver
Works to ensure that America's children have a healthy start by addressing issues such as health insurance, child care, child safety, and moral education.

Every Child Matters
http://everychildmatters.gov.uk
Conducts polls, publishes reports, works with reporters and state children's groups, runs advertising, and conducts campaigns on behalf of children. They have sponsored initiatives related to child abuse prevention, health insurance, after-school programs, and early childhood education.

Parent Television Council
http://parentstv.org
Works to ensure responsible programming for children and families. This Web site provides the general public information and opportunities to get involved in national lobbying campaigns.

Tobacco-Free Kids
http://tobaccofreekids.org
Works to support a tobacco-free environment for children through education and lobbying activities. The Web site provides opportunities for individuals to get involved in these campaigns.

Child Labor Coalition
http://stopchildlabor.org
Serves as a national network for the exchange of information about child labor, provides a forum and a unified voice on protecting working minors and ending child labor exploitation, and promotes progressive initiatives.

---

members of a team, or in family groups. Volunteers can provide direct service to others or supply important behind-the-scene services to an agency. Volunteer opportunities can also be "virtual," that is, performed at home via the Internet.

Short-Term Volunteerism

Volunteer assignments can be short-term, one-time-only commitments. That is, volunteers serve to resolve a specific issue. You may learn about these opportunities from the newspaper or flyers posted in your community. If the opportunity matches your ideals and your time schedule, you show up the day of the event and offer your services. For example, you could volunteer to clean up a neighborhood park or playground and in doing so improve the quality of play-life in that community. Or, you could volunteer to serve refreshments at an all-day immunization clinic that is being held at a local mall. Or, you could volunteer to hand out flyers on Election Day for a favored candidate that supports children and family issues that you believe in. The advantages of short-term volunteerism are that you can support different issues at different times and easily fit volunteerism into your schedule. Figure 10.4 suggests ways to advocate for children and families through short-term volunteerism.

Long-Term Volunteerism

Some people prefer to serve as a long-term volunteer for a not-for-profit agency whose mission they believe in. These volunteers stick to the same work schedule or job assignment for a long period of time. For example, you may volunteer every Tuesday from 3:30 p.m. to 6:00 p.m tutoring

Figure 10.4 Short-Term Volunteer Activities

1. Take a few trash bags and a box of disposable gloves to the neighborhood park and pick up litter. You will need quite a few bags because others will want to join in. Advocacy is contagious!
2. Give the caregivers of a chronically ill child a break. Stop by their home with some books and games and entertain the child for an hour or so.
3. Host a group of neighborhood parents to discuss common issues related to safety in the neighborhood.
4. Take a walk on a beautiful day and distribute "Get out the Vote" flyers.
5. Do a Web search for information about childhood safety issues. Share an interesting article with five friends who are parents.
6. Write a letter to the editor about the need for quality child care in your community. Send it to the local paper.
7. Log on to a Web site that offers legislative alerts (like www.naeyc.org) and send instant e-mail to your legislator giving your opinion about an upcoming bill.
8. Send that legislative alert to five friends. Let them know what kind of legislation is being discussed in your state.
9. Collect your coffee money for a week, buy a great toy or game, and drop it off at a not-for-profit child care center or take it to the pediatric unit of the local hospital.
10. Boycott a restaurant that does not offer a smoke-free environment for children and families.

youngsters at an after-school program sponsored by the YMCA. Or, you might choose to work the same hours every week for a particular program, but the work you would do during those hours may vary. Remember Janelle who works at Ronald McDonald House? This is the kind of volunteer work she does. She has a set schedule, but her duties vary from week to week.

The advantage of long-term volunteering to agencies is that they can rely on having "man power" available at scheduled times. The advantage for the volunteer is that she has a consistent routine, gains firsthand knowledge about issues, learns new skills, and develops confidence in her ability to make a difference for children and families.

Team

Many people like to volunteer as a team (Cravens, 2004). They can be employees from a particular company, members of a club or association, or a group of friends who want to spend time together while engaged in a worthwhile activity. For example, a group of four college students, who happen to love both children and horses, volunteer at a local equestrian center one Saturday each month. They help children with special needs who, under the guidance of a physical therapist, learn to ride horses. The college students are able to satisfy their longing to be around horses, learn valuable skills related to working with children with special needs, and advocate for the inclusion of children with special needs into typical childhood activities. These students are engaged in a long-term volunteer commitment.

Team volunteering can also be short term. For example, a team of kindergarten teachers decide to spend a Saturday leading art activities for young children who, with their parents, attend a one-day fund-raising event sponsored by the community's arts council. The teachers enjoy working together and getting to know each other outside the context of the classroom while supporting a good cause—bringing art into the life of a community.

Family

Family volunteering is also a possibility. It can involve the whole family, one child and one parent, or several siblings and an extended family

Bob Nichols/USDA/NRCS/Natural Resources Conservation Service

When families volunteer together, children learn that service to others is important and fulfilling.

member (Ellis, 2004). One advantage of family volunteering is that parents spend quality time with their children and get to see their children's strengths in a new context. Children learn, firsthand, about issues that face other children and families in their community. They also develop the disposition to be an advocate. Of course, not all volunteer activities will be appropriate for all children. Family members will need to carefully investigate the potential of volunteer opportunities before they sign on.

Direct Service

Direct Service volunteers work directly with clients of service organizations. They might tutor children in literacy development at local schools. They might drive young children and their families to doctor or dentist appointments. They might distribute food at food banks or clothing at shelters. Or, they might read to children who are hospitalized with chronic illnesses.

However, some people like to work behind the scene and perform vital tasks that support the mission of the agency. They might research facts to use in the development of an agency's advocacy material, or shop for supplies for a fund-raising event. They could stuff envelopes for a mail campaign, or restock shelves of a community distribution center.

Virtual

Lack of transportation, or a home-based obligation, such as a chronically ill family member, may have prevented some people from supporting causes through advocacy in the past, but with the advent of the home computer and the World Wide Web, everyone can find a way to be a volunteer advocate. **Virtual volunteers** complete tasks online from a home computer.

The benefit of virtual volunteerism to agencies is that it expands their volunteer program by allowing people who otherwise could not volunteer the opportunity participate (ServiceLeader.org, 2004). The benefit to the volunteer is that it allows a great amount of flexibility in scheduling tasks. Examples of virtual volunteer tasks include online research to gather information to use in writing a grant proposal, providing professional consulting expertise, preparing information for a Web site, keeping track of legislation that could affect an agency's clients, and preparing legislative alerts to be sent via e-mail.

FINDING OPPORTUNITIES

Opportunities to volunteer and advocate for causes that you believe in are limitless. Anyone who wants to be an advocate for an issue that affects young children and their families will find an opportunity that will fit his interests, skills, and schedules. But how do you find the right opportunity? Where do you start? The best place to start is in your local community where you will be able to witness firsthand the effects of your efforts.

Most communities have an agency that recruits and places volunteers in community service agencies. Look in the telephone book under volunteer centers. Also read the local newspaper. There may be a weekly column that outlines service opportunities and gives contact information. Call your local paper to get more information about this column. If they don't have one, you might volunteer to write one and focus on services that benefit young children and their families.

Look for articles in community newsletters that tell of forthcoming community or fund-raising events. There is always a need for volunteers to work at these functions. You can also find volunteer opportunities by checking with your local United Way organization, the YMCA, the library, and community groups that support ideals you believe in.

The Internet provides many ways for you to find volunteer opportunities. For example, The Points of Light Foundation Index contains links to major regional and nationwide sites in the United States and Canada that provide updated lists of volunteer opportunities at various different organizations. Community Networks and FreeNets often have areas to promote local volunteer/service initiative and work in conjunction with local volunteer centers. Figure 10.5 describes Web sites that promote volunteer opportunities in the United States and Canada.

Figure 10.5 Volunteer Opportunities in the United States and Canada

---

Points of Light Foundation
http://www.pointsoflight.org
Maintains an index of volunteer centers to help mobilize people and resources to find creative solutions to community problems. Visitors to this site can link to volunteer centers in their own communities to find opportunities to work for children and families.

The Organization for Community Networks
http://ofcn.org
Maintains a listing of networks and FreeNets by nation and state.

Break Away: The Alternative Break Collection
http://alternativebreaks.org
Promotes service on the local, regional, national, and international levels through break-oriented programs that immerse students in different cultures, heighten social awareness, and advocate life-long social action.

Charity Village Volunteer Bulletin Board
http://charityvillage.com
Registered Canadian charities and public service agencies needing volunteers may post a notice on the Charity Village Bulletin Board.

Hands on Network
http://www.handsonnetwork.org
Brings people together to strengthen communities through meaningful action. It is made up of over 55 national and international volunteer organizations that act as entrepreneurial civic action centers. Visitors to the site can find a starting point for volunteerism by choosing from a variety of projects that connect community needs with their time and interests.

(continued)

Volunteer Match
http://www.volunteermatch.org
Provides a way to search via zip code to find a listing of projects that fit the volunteer's description.

Make a Difference Day
http://www.usaweekend.com/diffday/
Includes a database of volunteer opportunities for Make a Difference Day, which is held each October.

Volunteer Solutions
http://www.volunteersolutions.org
Hosts a database of volunteer opportunities in selected cities in the United States.

Volunteers of America
http://www.voa.org
Offers more than 160 different programs that help people including children, youth, the elderly, families in crisis, the homeless, people with disabilities or mental illness, and ex-offenders returning to society.

Volunteer Canada
http://www.volunteer.ca/
Provides a list of over 200 volunteer centers serving communities across Canada.

EVALUATING VOLUNTEER OPPORTUNITIES

Once you have found a volunteer opportunity that sounds interesting, you will need to evaluate it to make sure it fits your interests and skills. A first step is to visit the site to get a sense of the overall environment and obtain more information about the position. Ask for a written brochure that describes the agency and its mission. Also ask for a written description of the position or clarification of the following points:

- What is the nature, scope, and purpose of the position?
- What are the duties, responsibilities, and tasks involved?
- What skills are needed to do the job?
- What training is available?
- Who supervises the activities?
- What amount of time would be required? (Number of hours per week and length of commitment)

After researching the volunteer site, take the second step in evaluating a potential volunteer opportunity by reflecting on your own qualifications and interests as they relate to the job description. Ask yourself:

■ Are you supportive of the mission of the agency?
■ Will the assignment challenge you but not overwhelm you?
■ Will you have opportunities to utilize the skills you have while learning new skills that will be helpful to you in the future?
■ Is the amount of time required realistic?
■ Will you have the opportunity to take on more responsibility when you are ready?
■ Do you feel comfortable in the setting and with the clients and other volunteers?

When you are comfortable that your interests, skills, and schedule match the agency's expectation, it is time to make a formal application. In cases where direct service to clients or a long-term commitment is a part of the volunteer's responsibilities, expect there to be a screening process involving an in-depth interview, reference check, and even a background check. Know that the agency is as interested in making a good match as you are. Volunteers who are confident in their duties feel they are making a difference for others, and are comfortable with the people they work with on a daily basis make long lasting commitments to the program.

FULFILLING RESPONSIBILITIES

When you commit to a position as a volunteer, people count on you. Even though the term *volunteer* implies free choice, you have taken on a commitment that carries multiple responsibilities. As a volunteer, you have the responsibility to:

■ Keep your commitments and be on time. Notify your supervisors as early as possible when you need to be absent or you plan to leave your position.
■ Be a good manager of your own time and energy. Arrive at the work site refreshed and ready to give all you can. Your commitment and enthusiasm will energize the environment and model a positive attitude to all involved.
■ Understand your role and what the agency expects of you. Follow the organization's policies and guidelines. Take initiative but don't overstep your authority. Ask for clarification when you need it.

- Do your best work. Utilize all your skills in every task you do. Go beyond what is expected. Finish the task you are assigned—don't leave things for others to do unless they are expecting to pick up where you left off.
- Be a team player. Respect everyone's unique contribution. Step up and lead when you need to. Fall back and take another's lead when it will facilitate getting the job done.
- Demonstrate good judgment. Think before you speak and think before you act. Be sensitive. The people you are working with may have very different life experiences than you. Put yourself in the other person's shoes and appreciate their core knowledge.
- Maintain the confidentiality of the clients and agencies you work with. Be discreet. Be loyal.
- Learn from your activities. Stretch yourself. Take advantage of every opportunity you have to increase your understanding of issues that face children and families.

Being a reliable and committed volunteer and working with agencies that support young children and their families is very rewarding. Not only are you able to take a stand for issues that concern you, but you learn new skills while in the process of helping others.

SUMMARY

Volunteers are people who donate time and energy to support causes they believe in. Volunteerism can be a short-term or long-term commitment to a program. It can be an individual endeavor or performed in team or even family units. Opportunities to volunteer are easy to find. Most communities have volunteer centers that list possibilities in the community. There are also many Web sites that seek to match volunteers with the right program. Good volunteers are dedicated and committed individuals who truly make a difference in the lives of young children and their families.

RELEVANT CONCEPTS

volunteers

family volunteering

direct service volunteers

virtual volunteers

FOR FURTHER READING

Anna's Story: A Journey of Hope by Jenna Bush, 2007. Published by HarperCollins Publishers.

Giving: How Each of Us Can Change the World by Bill Clinton, 2007. Published by Alfred A. Knopf.

LINKS TO ADVOCACY RESOURCES

Voices for America's Children

http://www.voicesforamericaschildren.org/

Voices for America's children is devoted to enhancing state and local child advocacy organizations. It provides resources and training for developing advocacy skills, research on issues relating to children's well-being, legislative alerts, and reviews of current and pending legislation.

Safer Child

http://www.saferchild.org

A nonprofit educational information and referral resource on all issues of child welfare, child health, and child safety.

Alliance for Children and Families

http://www.alliance1.org/

An international membership association representing more than 350 private, nonprofit child- and family-serving organizations.

QUESTIONS FOR REFLECTION AND DISCUSSION

1. Share with others information about the volunteer or service work you have done in the past. What did you learn about people and about your community from this work? What skills did you gain?

2. Review the Profile of an Advocate at the beginning of this chapter. Develop a list of skills Amanda Redford needed to become a successful CASA volunteer. How do those skills support her work as a teacher? Or, how do the skills she has learned as a teacher aid her volunteer efforts? Does the kind of volunteer work she engages in appeal to you?

3. Discuss how you might find volunteer opportunities that relate to a specific issue you believe in.

ADVOCACY IN ACTION: APPLICATION ACTIVITIES

1. Plan and carry out a short-term individual or group advocacy project in your community. Document the event through journal entries, photographs, and reflections. Share your experience with classmates. Be sure to link your volunteerism to advocacy efforts.

2. Using one of the Web sites listed in Figure 10.5, find a volunteer opportunity in your community. Contact the agency and find out more information about the expectations of the position. Evaluate the position to see how it matches your interests and skills. Report your findings and reflect on whether this would be a feasible project for you to do.

3. Read the local newspaper each day for one week and cut out items that might lead to opportunities to advocate for children through volunteering. Analyze three of the opportunities you find by asking yourself such questions as: What type of commitment is required? What skills would be involved? What issues would you be supporting? What opportunity would you have to learn? Share your findings with your class.

Appendix: Advocacy Planning Worksheet

Strategic Plan for Advocacy	
Date Initiated	**Advocacy Group or Individual**
Statement of the Problem	
Background Information	
Objective	
Barriers	
Stakeholders and Their Perspectives	

Constituents	Allies	Opponents

Primary Targets for Advocacy	Secondary Targets for Advocacy

Long-Term Goals	Short-Term Goals

Networks and Coalitions You Can Work With

Educational Tactics	Persuasive Tactics	Mobilization Tactics

Timeline

References

Alvarado, A. (2003). *The United States' nonprofit sector*. Washington, DC: National Non-profit Association.

American Academy of Pediatrics. (2001). Committee on children with disabilities policy statement: Developmental surveillance and screening of infants and young children, *Pediatrics, 108,* 192–196.

Amidei, N. (2002). *So you want to make a difference: Advocacy is the difference* (14th ed.). Washington, DC: OMB Watch.

Bardes, B., Shelley, M. D., & Schmidt, S. (2006). *American government and policies today: The essentials* (2006–2007 ed.). Belmont, CA: Thomson Wadsworth.

Benson, P. (2000). *EMSC's role in shaping policy: A practical guide to changing minds and saving lives*. Washington, DC: Emergency Medical Services for Children (EMSC) National Resource Center.

Berger, E. H. (2000). *Parents as partners in education* (5th ed.). Upper Saddle River, NJ: Merrill/Prentice Hall.

Bigelow, B., & Peterson, B. (Eds.). (2002). *Rethinking globalization: Teaching for justice in an unjust world*. Milwaukee, WI: Rethinking Schools Press.

Bredekamp, S., & Copple, C. (Eds.). (1997). *Developmentally appropriate practice in early childhood programs* (Rev. ed.). Washington, DC: National Association for the Education of Young Children.

Chalk, R., Gibbons, A., & Scarupa, H. J. (2002). *The multiple dimensions of child abuse and neglect: New insights into an old problem*. Washington, DC: Child Trends. Retrieved April 27, 2007, from www.childtrends.org/Files/ChildAbuseRB.pdf

Cheadle, D., & Prendergast, J. (2007). *Not on our watch: The mission to end genocide in Darfur and beyond*. New York: Hyperion.

Child Help. (2007). *Signs of child abuse*. Retrieved September 17, 2007, from http://www.childhelp.og/signs-of-child-abuse

Child Welfare Information Gateway. (2006). *Long-term consequences of child abuse and neglect factsheet*. Retrieved September 16, 2007, from http://www.childwelfare.gov/pubs/factsheets/long_term_consequences.cfm

Clinton, W. J. (2007). *Giving: How each of us can change the world*. New York: Knopf.

Connolly, P., Hayden, J., & Levin, D. (2007). *From conflict to peace building: The power of early childhood initiatives, lessons from around the world*. Redmond, WA: World Forum Foundation.

Cook, R. E., Klein, M. D., & Tessier, A. (2008). *Adapting early childhood curricula for children with special needs* (7th ed.). Upper Saddle River, NJ: Merrill/Prentice Hall.

References

Copple, C., & Bredekamp, S. (2008). Getting clear about developmentally appropriate practice. *Young Children, 63*(1), 54–55.

Cravens, J. (2004). Tips for group volunteering. Austin, TX: RGK Center for Philanthropy. Retrieved April 27, 2006, from http://www.serviceleader.org/new/volunteers/article/2004/03/000216print.php

de Benedictis, T., Jaffe, J., & Segal, J. (2007). *Child abuse: Types, signs, symptoms, causes, and help.* Retrieved September 17, 2007, from http://www.helpguide.org/mental/child_abuse_physical_emotional_sexual_neglect.htm

Decker, C. A., & Decker, J. R. (2005). *Planning and administering early childhood programs* (8th ed.). Upper Saddle River, NJ: Merrill/Prentice Hall.

Ellis, S. J. (2004). Volunteering with your family. Philadelphia, PA: Energize, Inc. Retrieved April 27, 2006, from http://www.serviceleader.org/new/volunteers/articles/2003/04/000059print.php

Feeney, S., & Freeman, N. K. (1999). *Ethics and the early childhood educator: Using the NAEYC Code.* Washington, DC: National Association for the Education of Young Children.

FirstSigns.org. (2007). *Sharing concerns.* Retrieved September 18, 2007, from http://www.firstsigns.org/concerns/sharing.htm

Fox, M. (2001). *Reading magic: Why reading aloud to our children will change their lives forever.* New York: Harcourt.

Freeman, N. K., & Feeney, S. (2004). The NAEYC Code is a living document. *Young Children, 59*(6), 12–16.

Friedrich, M. J. (2007). Jeffrey Sachs, PhD: Ending extreme poverty, improving the human condition. *Journal of the American Medical Association, 298,* 1849–1859. Retrieved July 18, 2007, from http://jama.ama.org/cgi/contert/full/298/16/1849

Gay-Straight Alliance Network. (2008). *Developing strategies.* Retrieved January 18, 2008, from http://www.gsanetwork.org/resources/strategies/html

Glascoe, F. P. (1999). Using parents' concerns to detect and address developmental behavior problems. *Journal of Society of Pediatric Nurses, 4,* 24–35.

Goffin, S. G., & Lombardi, J. (1988). *Speaking out: Early childhood advocacy.* Washington, DC: National Association for the Education of Young Children.

Gonzalez-Mena, J. (2007). *50 early childhood strategies for working and communicating with diverse families.* Upper Saddle River, NJ: Merrill/Prentice Hall.

HelpGuide.org. (2007). *Child abuse: Types, signs, symptoms, causes and help.* Retrieved September 17, 2007, from http://www.helpguide,org/mental/child_abuse_physical_emotional_sexual_neglect.htm

Henniger, M. L. (2008). *Teaching young children: An introduction* (4th ed.). Upper Saddle River, NJ: Merrill/Prentice Hall.

Hyson, M. (Ed.). (2003). *Preparing early childhood professionals: NAEYC's standards for programs.* Washington, DC: National Association for the Education of Young Children.

International Reading Association. (2007). Advocacy manual. Retrieved March 7, 2007, from http://www.ira.org/association/advocacy

Jalongo, M. R., & Isenberg, J. P. (2000). *Exploring your role: A practitioner's introduction to early childhood education.* Upper Saddle River, NJ: Merrill/Prentice Hall.

Karr-Morse, R., & Wiley, M. S. (1997). *Ghosts from the nursery: Tracing the roots of violence.* New York: The Atlantic Monthly Press.

Kieff, J., & Casbergue, R. (2000). *Playful learning and teaching: Integrating play into preschool and primary programs.* Needham Heights, MA: Allyn & Bacon.

Knauer, K. (2007). *Global warming: The causes, the perils, the solutions, the actions: What you can do.* New York: Time Inc. Home Entertainment.

Knitzer, J. K. (2007). *Testimony on the economic and societal costs of poverty.* Retrieved June 15, 2006, from http://www.nccp.org/publications'pub_705.html

Lewis, J., Jongsma, K. S., & Berger, A. (2005). *Educators on the frontline: Advocacy strategies for your classrooms, your school, and your profession.* Newark, DE: International Reading Association.

Lombardi, J. (2007). Early childhood development: A global movement. *Young Children, 62*(6), 10–11.

Moore, M. L., Howard, V. F., & McLaughlin, T. E. (2002). Siblings of children with disabilities: A review and analysis. *International Journal of Special Education, 17*(1), 49–64.

National Association for the Education of Young Children. (1996). *Position statement, Prevention of child abuse in early childhood programs and the responsibilities of early childhood professionals to prevent child abuse.* Retrieved May 10, 2008, from http://www.naeyc.org/about/positions/ pschab98.asp

National Association for the Education of Young Children. (2003). *Early childhood educators and child abuse prevention: NAEYC's perspective, research findings, and future actions.* Washington, DC: Author.

National Association for the Education of Young Children. (2004a). *Affiliate public policy tool kit.* Washington, DC: Author.

National Association for the Education of Young Children. (2004b). *Code of ethical conduct: Supplement for early childhood adult educators.* Washington, DC: Author.

National Association for the Education of Young Children. (2005). *Code of ethical conduct and statement of commitment.* Washington, DC: Author.

National Association for the Education of Young Children. (2006). *Code of ethical conduct: Supplement for early childhood program administrators.* Washington, DC: Author.

References

National Association for the Education of Young Children. (2007). *Making a difference: Excellence in early childhood education: Recommendations to the 110th U.S. Congress*. Washington DC: Author. Retrieved December 9, 2007, from www.naeyc.org

National Center for Children in Poverty. (2007). *Basic facts about low-income children: Birth to age 18*. New York: Author.

National Center for Children in Poverty. (2007). *Addressing the challenge*. Retrieved September 17, 2007, from http://nccp.org/about.html

Oxfam International. (2006). *Education for global citizenship: A guide for schools*. Retrieved January 18, 2008, from http://www.oxfam.org

Phillips, C. B. (1998). Preparing teachers to use their voices for change. *Young Children, 53*(3), 55–60.

Prevent Child Abuse America. (2007). *Recognizing child abuse: What parents should know*. Retrieved September 17, 2007, from www.preventchildabuse.org

Reckdahl, K. (2007). Crisis in child care. *The Times Picayune,* May 14.

Robinson, A., & Stark, D. R. (2002). *Advocates in action: Making a difference for young children*. Washington, DC: The National Association for the Education of Young Children.

Sachs, J. D. (2005). *The end of poverty: Economic possibilities for our time*. New York: Penguin Books.

Sandall, S., McLean, M. E., & Smith, B. J. (2000). *DEC recommended practices in early intervention/early childhood special education*. Denver, CO: Division of Early Childhood.

Seefeldt, C., & Barbour, N. (1997). *Early childhood education: An introduction* (4th ed.). Upper Saddle River, NJ: Merrill/Prentice Hall.

ServiceLeader.org. (2004). *What is virtual volunteering?* Austin, TX: RGK Center for Philanthropy. Retrieved April 27, 2006, from http://www.serviceleader.org/new/virtual/2003/04/000020print.php

Shultz, J. (2003). *The democracy owner's manual: A practical guide to changing the world*. San Francisco, CA: The Democracy Center.

Smith, S. K. (2006). *Mandatory reporting of child abuse and neglect*. Retrieved July 8, 2007, from http://www.smith-lawfirm.com/mandatory_reporting.htm

Thomlison, B. (2004). Child maltreatment: A risk factor and protective factors. In M. W. Fraser (Ed.), *Risk and resilience in childhood: An ecological perspective* (pp. 89–133). Washington, DC: National Association of Social Workers.

United Nations, Office of the High Commissioner for Human Rights (OHCHR). (1990). *Convention on the Rights of the Child*. Geneva, Switzerland: United Nations.

Wright, K., Stegelin, D. A., & Hartle, L. (2007). *Building family, school, and community partnerships* (3rd ed.). Upper Saddle River, NJ: Merrill/Prentice Hall.

Wright, P., & Wright, P. (Ed.). (2006). *From emotions to advocacy* (2nd ed.). Hartfield, VA: Harbor House Law Press.

Index

Index

Index

Index